A Dog's Best Friend

A Dog's Best Friend

An Activity Book for Kids and Their Dogs

Lisa Rosenthal

CHICAGO
REVIEW
PRESS

Library of Congress Cataloging-in-Publication Data

Rosenthal, Lisa, 1962–
    A dog's best friend : an activity book for kids and their dogs /
Lisa Rosenthal
        p.   cm.
    Includes bibliographical references (p. 162).
    Summary: Over fifty activities and crafts and dozens of sidebars
teach young children how to take care of their dogs while fostering
a deep, long-lasting bond between child and dog.
    ISBN 1-55652-362-9
    1. Dogs Juvenile literature.   2. Creative activities and seat work
Juvenile literature.   [1. Dogs 2. Handicraft.]   I. Title.
SF426.5.R665   1999   99-12455
636.70887—dc21   CIP

Cover and interior illustrations: © Bonnie Matthews
Cover and interior design: Mel Kupfer
The author and the publisher of this book disclaim all liability incurred in
connection with the use of the information contained in this book.

Published by Chicago Review Press, Incorporated
814 North Franklin Street
Chicago, Illinois 60610
ISBN 1-55652-362-9
Printed in the United States of America

5 4 3 2 1

for Ted, the best partner
and playmate of all

Contents

3

Safety First...........39

4

Nibbles & Treats..........75

Foreword

The relationship a child forges with a companion dog can last a lifetime. The friendship, the sharing, the bond will stay with that child well into adulthood. When reminiscing, many people naturally dwell upon a special dog friend they had as children. They may be purebred or mixed. They may be big and galumphing or small and spritely. They may be lazy, hyper, furry, slobbery, silly, or majestic. But in the end, they are *friends*.

Often, a dog is the first exposure a child has to the wider world of responsibility. Lessons of duty and commitment frequently come in the guise of a canine companion. Dogs depend upon people for all of the things they need to lead happy, healthy lives, and children can play an important part in their care.

A Dog's Best Friend is a wonderful guidebook to help children develop a friendship with their dogs through participation and understanding. The activities laid out in this book have been designed to maximize children's interactions with their pets. Some activities emphasize direct involvement, such as administering proper feeding or recognizing when vet care is required. Others, though, develop intangible—yet equally important—aspects of friendship such as sharing and discovery, with ideas ranging from creating appropriate gifts for a dog to learning about the history of dogs.

These activities are safe (when all directions are followed and under adult supervision) and will help to promote a deep, caring bond between children and their dogs. Such a bond is invaluable not only to the specific relationship between child and pet, but also to the development of the child's awareness of the needs of others, human and nonhuman alike. Compassion, caring, and kindness become happy accidents upon the path to friendship.

Take a moment. Peruse the book. See the many ways in which a child can enhance his or her understanding of a pet. Participate in the activities with a child. Then, see that child develop a friendship and memories that will last a lifetime.

—John Caruso, director of humane education,
The Anti-Cruelty Society

 xi

Introduction for Parents

Kids and dogs is a great mix! Having a pet puppy or dog provides a regular source of fun and exercise for your kids—without carpooling and with no assembly or batteries required! Caring for an animal can teach kids many valuable lessons including

- **Responsibility** from taking care of the animal,

- **Patience** from training and playing games with the animal,

- **Confidence** from teaching the animal tricks,

- **Leadership** from remembering to provide for the dog's needs, and

- **Satisfaction** from a job well done.

Kids will have fun and at the same time develop a positive self-image.

A Dog's Best Friend is written with the belief that regular healthy interaction between a kid and her dog will lead to good care for the animal while teaching valuable life lessons. Activities are designed to keep kids involved with their four-legged pals after the initial excitement is over. Your kid will find fun games to play with his dog and cool things to make for his four-legged friend. Most of the activities require only household items and a little imagination; many can be done individually. Adult help is suggested for those activities that require the use of the oven or tools.

Good pet-care tips and information, collected from pet-care professionals and extensive research, are included as well. Appendix 1 provides a valuable children's reading list provided by The Anti-Cruelty Society. You'll find books about dogs, cats, owls, and other animals that will teach kids about caring for their new four-legged friend, help them to deal with the loss of a pet, offer great adventure tales, and more. Appendix 2 is a resource section that provides the addresses of animal-friendly Web sites, cable stations, and organizations that can provide you with more information or additional fun animal time.

Checklist of Considerations Before Bringing a Dog Home

A dog is a constant, loyal, unconditional friend for your child. However, there are a number of important things to consider before bringing a dog into your household.

1. Think about your lifestyle, your family, and your finances. Any animal that you adopt will require a long-term commitment from you and everyone else in the household. It's a commitment that should last for your dog's lifetime.

2. Talk with everyone in your home before adopting a pet. This is the time when you're likely to find out who your pet-care helpers will be and who won't be helping.

3. How many hours a day is your house empty? Puppies can be adopted as young as seven or eight weeks old, but such young creatures need to develop self-confidence so that they will interact in healthy ways with kids and other household members. This confidence is built by not leaving the puppy alone for long periods of time and giving him a lot of attention and even a few short obedience training sessions where your puppy can receive much-needed praise. Training problems (such as chewing on things you don't want him to) may develop if the dog is left home alone too often.

 Healthy Hound Hint

Many pet-care professionals suggest that you keep your dog indoors and make him part of your family.

4. Is an adult in the household willing to provide the obedience training—including socializing, behavioral training, and house training—to make the addition of a puppy to your home a good choice?

5. What kind of time do you have available for a dog? Are you home a lot but work out of your home so that you're not readily available?

6. Do you have young kids who are not in school? Are the kids older?

7. What is your family's activity level? Do you like to sit and read books? Watch TV? Or is your family very active, and do they enjoy a lot of physical activity? If you are a low-activity crowd, don't adopt a dog who requires a lot of physical exercise, such as a greyhound. Instead, think about adopting a breed like a basset hound. They enjoy a lot of relaxing, too.

8. How do you want to interact with a dog? Do you want a dog who's going to give a lot of affection or one who's more independent?

9. Do you want a small, medium, or large dog?

10. Do you want a male or female dog? Male dogs tend to be larger, eat more, and be more independent and therefore more difficult to obedience train. They are also more likely to fight. Female dogs tend to be easier to manage and are gentler. (These are generalizations, and early environmental influences—such as loud noises and physical abuse—and breeding will also affect the personality of individual dogs.) Neutering (male) or spaying (female) will mellow some of these sex-specific attributes.

Once You Have Made the Decision to Get a Dog

Once you take account of how you and your family members spend your time, you can search for a breed whose temperament matches your lifestyle. Here are some additional hints to help you in this decision-making process.

• If you're thinking of adopting an older dog, consider the age of the animal as compared to his average life span. This will indicate how well the animal will adjust to a new home environment. A dog in the early part of his life can be easier to train than one who has had time to develop bad habits, and, as with people, longtime habits are hard to break. However, keep in mind that puppies are the most challenging to train because they require the most effort, patience, and expertise.

- Don't read breed-specific books when you're hunting for a breed of dog who suits your lifestyle. Such books are for people who have already decided on a breed, so they are written with this in mind to help you enjoy your choice. Also, don't rely on breeders to give you unbiased information, because they love the breed they raise—otherwise they wouldn't be in the business.

Here are some books to help your investigation:

Benjamin L. Hart. *The Perfect Puppy: How to Choose Your Dog by Its Behavior.* New York: W. H. Freeman and Company, 1988.
Michele Lowell. *Your Purebred Puppy: A Buyer's Guide.* New York: Henry Holt and Company, Inc., 1990.

Chris Walkowicz. *The Perfect Match: A Buyer's Guide to Dogs.* New York: Simon & Schuster Macmillan, 1996.

- Shelters are great places to find companion animals. There is a tremendous overpopulation of dogs and cats in the United States. You can help reduce this problem by giving a slightly used dog (or cat) a new home. Not only can you find many loving animals at shelters, but they're a good value, too. Most shelters give an adopted animal all the appropriate vaccinations, provide spay or neutering operations, and even give you start-up supplies, often valued at hundreds of dollars, all for a small fee. Also, you may be surprised to learn that shelters are great, inexpensive places to find many purebred dogs without the purebred price.

Involve Kids from the Beginning

Involve your kids as much as possible when you are deciding on what type of dog to get. You want your kids to feel that they're a part of this decision, too. Also, involving your kids now will help you keep them involved later when the dog that they helped pick needs to be bathed or fed.

Once you pick out a dog, let your kid participate in decisions concerning the dog. This will help her take responsibility and give her the opportunity to teach you some things about your dog or reveal something about her that you didn't already know. Here are some suggestions.

1. Take your child shopping and let her pick out dog food with your help. This is a great time to teach your child a lesson in proper nutrition. Read the ingredients label together. (Note: There are no federal regulations requiring dog food labels that include such words as "ultra premium," "gourmet," and "natural" to contain any different or higher-quality ingredients than regular dog food. Compare ingredients labels to see what foods truly provide better nutrition. Also, you can ask your veterinarian or pet-care professional for her recommendations.)

2. Let your child pick out toys for the dog. You'll find helpful tips on good, safe toys throughout this book.

3. If your child is older, he can attend obedience training classes with the dog or at least help prac-tice the obedience lessons. Children as young as eight can successfully help train a dog depending on the child's physical strength, maturity, and confidence and the size of the dog. To obedience train without an adult's help, a child should be about 12. (Note: A puppy who is 12 weeks old is ready for obedience training. If you adopt a dog from a shelter, wait a couple of weeks for the dog to develop a sense of security and comfort in his new home before starting obedience training. However, if the dog tries to nip anyone, start training immediately.)

4. Buying a child a pet as a gift is *not* a good idea unless you involve the child in this decision. By including the child, the gift won't be a surprise, but you won't get any unwanted surprises once the dog has been added to your family.

What Breeds Mix Well with Kids?

It's difficult to say that specific breeds of dogs are better with kids than others. Just as people all in one family do not behave the same, there are personality variations within breeds of dogs. You may find a docile German shepherd or a combative cocker spaniel.

In general, a dog's personality is apparent after about six weeks and is the result of interacting with his mother and the other puppies in the litter. A dog's temperament is shaped over a few years and depends on how the dog interacts with others. Wherever you choose to get your dog, take the time to make sure that you're a good match. After all, this is a friendship that will last many years.

Once you settle on a particular breed or a mixed breed, take the time to let your child interact with the specific animal you are considering. It's important to see how your child reacts with a particular dog. Some dogs have an easygoing temperament and will adapt well to a new home with children. If the dog interacts with your child with little fear or hesitation, this is a good sign of an easygoing temperament.

Buying an animal from a responsible breeder or adopting one from an animal shelter is a better idea than buying an animal from a newspaper ad. Buying from a dog-breeding professional or adopting from a shelter is buying from people who know about the dog. They will provide the proper care and

---

 Good News

Many animal behaviorists now believe that human handling (but only a limited amount) of newborn puppies is healthy, as it can help them become better problem solvers, more self-confident in competitive situations with other dogs, and more attracted to people.

Limit gentle handling to no more than 10 minutes a day and always supervise your child when she is handling a very young pup. A child should be sitting when first handling a puppy. Puppies may playfully nip, and this way the child cannot drop the puppy.

If your puppy is eight weeks old or older, more handling is not only OK, it is essential and feels good, too—for both of you.

socialization training that will help the dog learn to live in a new loving household. Getting a free puppy out of the paper is tricky because you won't know this dog's temperament or potential for developing a health problem; for example, if its mother was bred with another animal too closely related. Also, getting a dog from a friend can be difficult, especially when the mix doesn't quite work out the way you planned.

What to Do When You Bring a New Baby Home into a House Where a Dog Already Lives

If you treat your dog like a baby substitute, your dog is not likely to respond positively to this new creature in your home that is getting more attention while he's getting less. Because dogs are pack animals, all the attention to this new family member will indicate to the dog that the baby is higher up in the pack hierarchy. Your dog won't think that the baby deserves this higher position because the baby can't even move around on his own. It's possible that your dog may try to nip or bite at the baby to get his position back.

By planning ahead you can help insure a safe and healthy relationship between your pet and new baby. Ask your veterinarian how to properly introduce the new baby to your existing pet. Your dog can learn that the baby is a good thing because someone will always be home (at least for a while) and there will be more visitors, too.

 ## Make Your Home a No-Yelling Zone

One reason kids are bitten by dogs more often than adults is because kids sometimes scream, and screaming excites dogs. Also, a dog's sense of hearing is far more acute than our own, so a scream that sounds loud to us is even louder to him. Teach your kids never to yell near your dog.

If you bring an older child into your home, let the child feed the dog and give him clean water, initially with your help and then on his own. This will teach the dog that the child is a good caretaker, to be respected for the things he provides.

With proper care a dog will add a lot of joy to your home. A dog is a good rainy-day pal or a friend to play with in the sun. By doing a little planning and taking some careful first steps, you and your child will have a pal for a very long time.

 The Foster Care Option

If you're not sure if you and your child are ready to make the 12- to 15-year commitment to be pet owners, call your local shelter for information about a foster care program. Many shelters need safe, clean homes for dogs to recover from an injury. This can be a short-term commitment of as little as a few weeks.

Foster care can give you a chance to test drive dog ownership by seeing how other family members react to an animal in the home. Also, foster care is flexible—either you are or are not available to help at a particular time.

Most shelters require foster care volunteers to complete an orientation program before allowing them to care for one of their animals. But beware: these animals can grab onto your heart and make it tough to let them go.

Introduction for Kids

Wouldn't it be great to have a friend who's always ready to play, lives close by, and doesn't need to go home before dark? Well, if you have a dog or are thinking of getting one, that's exactly what you have! Dogs are great companions, playmates, and friends. All he asks for in return is some regular playtime with you and to be cared for properly by you and other members of your family. Pretty good deal, don't you think?

A Dog's Best Friend is filled with fun things to do and make, good care tips, and interesting facts about dogs. Whether you're training him to sit, baking peanut butter yummies for him, playing Frisbee together, or burying bones, you'll find tons of ways to show your dog you love him and have fun, too.

A Dog's Best Friend

Puppy Love

Your family has decided to adopt or buy a puppy—
what a wonderful new addition to the family!
Your puppy will be a fun playmate. All he asks
is to be properly cared for and loved by you
and other members of your family.

Shop City

L ove and attention are two very important ingredients for a successful puppy welcoming party. Here's a shopping list of items that you will also need to buy, borrow, or find to make your puppy feel right at home.

- Crate or kennel
- Crate pad or blanket
- Food bowl
- Water dish
- Safe toys (See Chapter 5 for a list of safe toys.)

- Collar
- Leash
- ID tags
- Nail clippers
- Flea comb
- Canine toothbrush
- Puppy shampoo
- Bottle of household cleaning fluid (for accidents)
- You and time to play

 Play It Safe

Some cities and towns have guidelines for what constitutes an adequate animal shelter. Check your local city laws to see if your area has any restrictions.

Puppy's First Day at Home

When you first bring your puppy home, he'll be nervous because he's in a new place and there are so many new people, voices, objects, and rooms to explore. If you are patient and tender, your puppy will learn quickly to feel comfortable in his new home. Here's a list of dos and don'ts for that first day.

Do

* Do introduce your puppy to one person at a time.
* Do let your puppy explore one room at a time. Breaking down a large space like a house into individual rooms will help the little guy feel more comfortable.
* Do handle your puppy for a few minutes each hour, but otherwise let him explore freely. Do, each day, rub her ears, tickle her belly, stroke her tail, and pick up her paws each day. This type of daily interaction will help your puppy become comfortable with accepting handling that will allow you to groom her now and later when she's an adult dog.
* Do pet him softly.
* Do give her food and water soon after your puppy has had some time to adjust to his new home.

Don't

* Don't make any loud noises or sudden movements around your puppy.
* Don't handle your puppy roughly.
* Don't try to train the little guy right away.
* Don't yell around your puppy.
* Don't squeeze, tug, toss, pull, or drag your puppy. She's your friend and needs to be treated with gentle care.

A dog is considered a puppy during his first year or two of life. During the first six months of your puppy's life, he or she will need to visit the veterinarian many times for vaccinations and neutering or spaying. It's very important that you take your puppy to the veterinarian to get vaccines that will help him grow up healthy and strong.

Going to the veterinarian can be stressful for a puppy. Ask your veterinarian to use ultrathin needles and room-temperature vaccines so your puppy won't learn that a trip to the vet means pain. Also, try offering your puppy a treat to divert attention away from the pinch of the needle. This is a good trick to try with older fearful dogs, too. (See Chapter 3 for some more tips to make a visit to the veterinarian less stressful.)

 Paws for Thought

When puppies are born they cannot see, hear, or smell. They are born with heat sensors.

Puppy Vaccination Chart

When you adopt a dog, ask for a record of the dog's inoculations (shots), including the dates, amounts, and types of medicine given. Ask if the puppy has a known medical history (such as an allergy) and if the puppy has been dewormed.

By eight weeks, puppies are ready for adoption. Before you take your puppy home, make an appointment to see your veterinarian so he can give the puppy an examination and any shots necessary to keep your new friend healthy.

You can keep track of your puppy's visits to the veterinarian and help your parents remember when it's time to go back by making a vaccination chart and keeping it on your refrigerator.

 Paws for Thought

Did you know dalmations
are pure white
when they are born?

 Paws for Thought

In young puppies, 95 percent of their immunity comes from *colostrum*, the milk the mother dog produces soon after giving birth.

5

Materials

* Plain white paper
* Puppy vaccination chart (below)
* Pencil
* Markers
* Magnet
* Highlighter

Directions

Place the white paper over the puppy vaccination chart and trace the outline of it. Next, write the words on this chart in the proper places. Decorate this chart with all kinds of things that your dog likes to play with, like a bone, a ball, you, and more. Use a magnet to hang this on the refrigerator. After every visit to the veterinarian, use the highlighter to mark off the visit and the shots your puppy received. Once you have the chart all filled in, you can celebrate with your puppy by going for a walk, playing in the yard, or giving him a new toy. After your puppy has his third round of shots, his immune system should be strong enough so that you can take him to meet other dogs.

PUPPY VACCINATION CHART						
Disease	Age at first vaccination (in weeks)	Date	Age at second vaccination (in weeks)	Date	Age at third vaccination (in weeks)	Date
Distemper*	6–10		10–12		14–16	
Infectious canine hepatitis* (CAV-1 or CAV-2)	6–8		10–12		14–16	
Parvovirus infection*	6–8		10–12		14–16	
Bordetella (kennel cough)*	6–8		10–12		14–16	
Parainfluenza (kennel cough)*	6–8		10–12		14–16	
Leptospirosis*	10–12		14–16		—	
Rabies	16		64		—	
Coronavirus*	6–8		10–12		12–14	

6

*Can be combined in one shot

As soon as your puppy comes home with you, he'll need a special place to sleep and a place to call his own. But until he is house trained, he can soil the bed and/or bedding. Here's a bed you can make from a cardboard box, and if your puppy soils it, you can make another one without too much trouble.

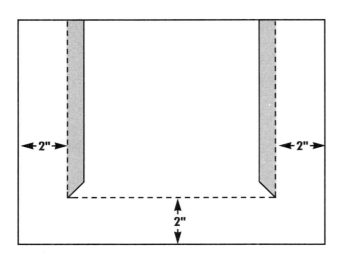

Materials

✳ 1 cardboard box, 2 to 3 times as big as your puppy
✳ Scissors
✳ Pencil
✳ Markers
✳ Soft towel or fleece blanket

Directions

Choose a cardboard box that is about two to three times the size of your puppy—just big enough for your puppy to feel safe but not so small that he won't feel comfortable. The box should be securely closed at the bottom. Use the scissors to cut off the top flaps of the box. Use the pencil to draw an entrance to the box that leaves at least two inches on each side and two inches or less on the bottom. (You may have to cut the bottom a little lower depending on the size of your puppy and what you think he can easily walk over.) Use the scissors to cut the box on the pencil lines

7

you've drawn. (Depending on how thick the card-board is, you may need help from an adult with this step.) Use the markers to decorate your dog's house and make it look like a brick house; dog house; castle; firehouse; or garden house filled with butterflies, birds, frogs, cats, goldfish, you, your family, and friends.

Once you've decorated your puppy's new bed, place the soft towel or blanket in the bottom of the box. Place the bed in a warm, quiet place not too close to any hallways or walkways. Fill up the bed with nice things your puppy will love.

- Try slipping a hot-water bottle under the blan-ket. This warmth will remind your puppy of the warmth of his brothers and sisters.

- Place a ticking clock under the blanket or close by. The ticking sound will remind your puppy of his mother's heartbeat.

- Leave a radio on all night. Low-volume sounds of music or a talk show will help keep your puppy comfortable.

- Place a food bowl and a water bowl nearby.

- One or two rubber toys are safe to leave with your puppy even when you're not in the room, as long as they're too large to be swallowed.

- Spread newspapers on the ground around the bed to catch accidents.

Housebreaking—teaching your puppy to go to the bathroom outside—can begin as young as 8 weeks, but puppies don't develop the muscles that control waiting to go to the bathroom until at least 16 weeks. It may then take 6 to 12 months to successfully develop these muscles to get your puppy house trained.

There are two ways to teach a puppy to go to the bathroom outside—crate training and paper training. A *crate* is a metal or plastic cage. You can make the crate a comfortable den by adding a soft blanket and a toy or two. The crate should be large enough for your puppy to stand up and walk around in. The crate is where your puppy should sleep, at least until he's housebroken. Dogs, even puppies, are less likely to go to the bathroom where they sleep, so this is already a big plus for this type of house training. Crate training is also just a two-step process to housebreaking your puppy—not in the crate, but outside. With paper training, you must teach your puppy to go on the paper and then transfer this learned behavior to only going to the bathroom outside.

Puppies need to go to the bathroom often—about once every two hours during the day and once every four hours at night. By about five months, your puppy should be able to wait the whole night before needing to go to the bathroom. So unless you or someone else stays home all day and sets an alarm to get up twice every night, your puppy will have accidents. This is a fact. Practice, consistency, and patience will get you a housebroken puppy.

The only time you can teach your puppy a housebreaking lesson is when you catch him going to the bathroom or *immediately* afterward. If your puppy goes to the bathroom inside the crate or when he's walking around the house,

say "no" in a firm but friendly voice, then immediately take him outside to a spot he's used before. Smelling this area will remind him that outdoors is the place to go to the bathroom. If he is inspired to go again at that point or anytime you are outside, be sure to give him a lot of praise. *Praise* is a way to tell your puppy he's done something good, something that pleases you. Say things like "good boy" and gently stroke his back and pet his head. Getting everyone else in your house to follow these house-training steps will help your puppy.

Puppies learn by:

- **Consistency**. Respond the same way every time.

- **Patience**. Don't get frustrated and walk away or yell.

- **Correction**. Say "no" and show your puppy what you want her to do.

- **Praise**. Let her know when she does something that pleases you.

If everyone follows the same house-training steps, it's just a matter of time before this job is done and it's time for fun!

Signs It's Time to Go

When your puppy needs to go to the bathroom, she'll show you at least two signs: she'll sniff the ground and she'll start walking in circles while sniffing because she's searching for a good spot to go.

Before your puppy starts giving you go signs, take her outside as soon as she wakes up and just after she finishes eating. You'll prevent some accidents this way. But let's face it, just as a baby is not potty-trained overnight, a puppy is going to have accidents. When your puppy has an accident in your home, clean the spot right away and apply an odor remover to the spot. This way she won't smell it and be tempted to go in the same spot again. And remember not to correct her unless you catch her going to the bathroom.

The World of Puppies

 eing good and kind and patient with your puppy is important because how you and other people interact with her now will shape her personality later. By the time your puppy is a full-grown adult dog, her personality is completely formed. Early puppy experiences affect her ability to interact with new dogs, interact with new people, learn, be emotionally stable, and be self-confident.

 Paws for Thought

Puppies can understand "come" and "stay" by 12 weeks of age with a lot of practice and praise.

How often and how much should you feed your puppy? It all depends on her age. Here's a chart to help you figure out how often your puppy pal gets to chow down.

ages	meals per day
Less than or equal to 3 months	4
3–6 months	3
6–9 months	2
Greater than or equal to 9 months	1–2

You should feed your puppy about as much food as she is able to eat in 15 to 20 minutes. If your puppy doesn't chow down as soon as the food's served, you can follow the puppy food package directions for the proper amount. However, this amount may be too much for your puppy. Some veterinarians recommend you cut the package quantity suggestion by one-third. Adjust the amount of food according to your puppy's age, weight, and activity level.

Throw a Puppy Party

During the first eight weeks of life, while your puppy is with her mother, she will learn a lot about how to play and fight by interacting with her littermates. But she won't learn everything before you adopt her. A puppy party is a fun way for you and your puppy to meet and play with other people and new dogs.

Materials
* Guest list
* People snacks
* Puppy and dog snacks
* Plenty of toys
* Planned activities

Directions
You can send out formal invitations or call friends and relatives on the phone and invite them over for a specific date and time. There are two kinds of puppy parties you can have. You can have a party where you introduce your puppy to your friends and relatives. This will give your puppy a chance to interact with people of all ages, sizes, and activity levels. Or you can invite a couple of friends and their dogs over and carefully introduce your puppy to each dog, one at a time. If you have this second kind of party, be sure to check with all the adults first to make sure they think this is a good idea. Also, it's very important that an adult be present during this kind of party just in case any of the guests become party poopers and don't play nicely. Look to your puppy for signs of stress to decide how much activity is appropriate.

Have plenty of snacks on hand for the guests— those with two and four legs! You can either have enough toys to share among the dog guests or you can have some games planned. (See Chapter 4 for some ideas.) If you share your puppy's toys, after the party wash them all in warm, soapy water

and thoroughly rinse them to get rid of the smells of the invited dogs. Remember that dogs use scent to distinguish what belongs to them. Washing off the other dogs' smells reintegrates the toy into your puppy's environment so that he knows it belongs to him.

Puppies are full of energy and curiosity. Everything is new to them, so they're always exploring. Before you know it, your puppy will be an adult dog. Once he's finished growing and he's house and obedience trained, you'll have even more fun.

 Greetings in Dog

When your dog meets another dog, she'll sniff the other dog to find out if the other dog is a female or male and to tell if the dog is friendly.

2

Creature Comforts

About 12,000 years ago dogs evolved from wolves. Dogs still maintain many of the same traits as their wolf ancestors. For example, like wolves, dogs are pack animals. In the wild, they travel in a group and always need a leader. The *leader* is the one dog who the other dogs have chosen to protect them and to keep them safe. Usually the leader is the oldest male dog. In your household, even if you have only one dog, your dog sees your family as his pack. The leader of your household pack may be the oldest male or the biggest and strongest person in your home.

This chapter is filled with fun things to make your dog comfortable in his new pack.

Make Room for a New Dog

If you're bringing a new dog into your home when you already have one, a little preparation will go a long way to help your new pal get along with your old buddy. Each dog should have her own bed, food and water bowls, and toys. Later, once they become more familiar and comfortable with each other, they may begin sharing, but let them have their own place and space at first.

On the first day you bring home your new dog, introduce him to the dog already in your home on neutral turf—someplace outdoors that doesn't already have your old dog's scent on it; in other words, *not* in your backyard. Make sure both dogs are on leash. Let them say hello to each other the doggy way by sniffing and smelling each other. Watch their body language and listen to the noises they make. If you hear any growling, try to distract each dog from the interaction and maybe take a short walk with your old buddy before trying again.

Until everyone in your house thinks that the dogs are comfortable with each other, keep them separated in your home when an adult is not around to play it safe. One possibility is to crate the new dog. This won't limit the movement of the dog already in your home, which wouldn't be fair, and it gives the new dog a safe place to be until the two dogs begin to get along.

 Family Trees

The origin of the golden retriever can be traced back to a Scottish estate called Guisachan in 1867 or 1868, when Lord Tweedmouth mated a male yellow retriever named Nous with a Tweed water spaniel named Belle. Do you think this beautiful dog would be so popular today if he were called a tweedmouth?

Weave a Comfy Rug

If your dog still enjoys her puppy bed, or if your dog prefers to sleep in her crate, you can make these dens more comfortable by making a comfy rug to place inside.

Materials

✻ 1 piece of cardboard as big as you want to make the rug (It's a good idea to measure the bottom of your dog's bed or crate so the rug will be large enough to completely cover the floor of the den.)
✻ Scissors
✻ Pencil
✻ Clean rags like old T-shirts and towels
✻ Needle
✻ Thread
✻ Masking tape

Directions

Cut out a piece of cardboard that matches the size of the rug you'd like to make. Draw ½-inch-long pencil marks one inch apart around the side edges of the cardboard. Use the scissors to cut through these marks. This will be your loom. Cut strips of fabric one to two inches wide and as long as each rag, T-shirt, or towel permits.

To make a braid, select three different colored strips. Use the needle and thread to sew the three strips together at the top. Now braid these three strips by following the pattern left side over, right side over left, new left side over, and so on. You can close the sewn end of the fabric strips in a drawer to hold it while you braid. This will also keep the braid from twisting. Once you've braided the length of the fabric strips, sew the three strips together at the open end to secure. Each braided strand should measure as long as the cardboard loom is wide. If a braid is too short, add another braid to it by following the steps above and then sewing the two braids together at one end.

When you have as many braids as you have notches in the cardboard, place the end of one braid through one notch and through the parallel notch on the opposite side of the loom. Secure the ends of the braids to the back of the cardboard with masking tape.

Once you've made enough braids to fill the horizontal notches of your loom, make braids to thread through your loom. These should be as long as your loom is tall. To figure out how many braids you need, lay the finished braids on top of your loom. When the loom is covered, make two

or three more because you will squeeze the braids together to eliminate any gaps in the rug.

To weave the rug, take one braid at a time and weave it over and then under each long braid of your loom. Each vertical braid should be woven in the opposite pattern as the one before it. For example, if you weave your first braid over then under then over, then weave your second braid under then over then under, and so on until the braid comes out the opposite side of the loom. After weaving a few braids, push them together to make your rug tight.

22

The notches in your loom will secure the braids.

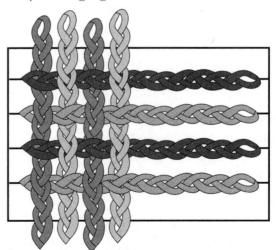

Push the braids together tightly.

Once you've woven all your braids and your loom is completely covered, use your needle and thread to sew and secure the ends of the braids to each side of the loom braids before removing the rug from the loom.

Now you're ready to place the rug in your dog's den. To encourage her, place a treat or her favorite toy on top of the rug. Once she starts to investigate the rug, she'll pick up your scent, and this will make her feel comfortable.

 ## Learning the Rules of the House

Don't expect your new dog to know the rules of your house. If you adopted a dog from the local shelter, remember that he lived in another house with possibly different rules. Your dog's previous owners might have spoken English or Spanish or Portuguese! So teach your dog the rules of your house with patience and kindness. Establish yourself as top dog, and enroll yourself and your dog in an obedience class. This will help you get along well from the start of your relationship, one that can last for a very long time.

 ## The Dog Who Loves Cats

Ginny, part schnauzer and part Siberian husky, who was rescued from a pound, walks the streets of her New York town at 4:30 A.M. every day with her owner, Philip Gonzalez. Ginny is an expert tracker and locator of stray cats. Philip finds homes for the stray cats Ginny finds. Together they've helped hundreds of cats find homes.

In November 1998, the Westchester Feline Club awarded Ginny their Cat of the Year Award for her good deeds.

Here's a comfy little treat that will help make your dog's bed feel more like a little home.

Materials
* ❋ 1 yard fabric
* ❋ Pencil
* ❋ Scissors
* ❋ Straight pins
* ❋ Needle
* ❋ Thread
* ❋ 100 percent polyester fiberfill

Directions
Turn fabric upside down on top of a table. Use the pencil to draw a dog bone. (Note: Draw the bone bigger than you want the pillow to be because you'll lose some of the pattern's size as you stitch a border, and stuffing will make the pillow wider but shorter, too.) Cut this pattern out. Use this first bone to draw the other side of the pillow. With the remaining fabric still upside down on the table,

place the cutout bone with the pattern side up on top of the remaining fabric and trace. Cut out this second bone.

To prepare to sew, place both patterned sides of the fabric facing each other so the unpatterned sides are facing out. Pin all the way around to hold the bones together while you sew. Double thread a needle (pull the thread through the needle's eye and pull it down about two feet, cut the thread at the spool, and knot the ends). Use a backstitch to securely sew the two pieces of fabric together, sewing about one-quarter inch from the outer edge of the fabric, and most of the way around the bone pattern.

Sew three and a half sides of the bone using the backstitch. Invert the fabric so that the pattern is now on the outside. Tear off little pieces of the polyester fiberfill, and stuff the bone starting at the farthest point and working back toward the hole opening. To get a very firm pillow, insert a lot of fiberfill; if you want a flatter lounging pillow, insert less fiberfill.

When finished stuffing the pillow, place straight pins around the opening to hold the fabric together as you finish sewing this last part. You can use a backstitch to finish closing the bone, or, for a neater appearance, you can fold in the outer edges of the fabric and sew tight little stitches on this doubled-over fabric. Place the pooch pillow in your dog's bed, and see how long it takes him to notice it and then fall asleep on it.

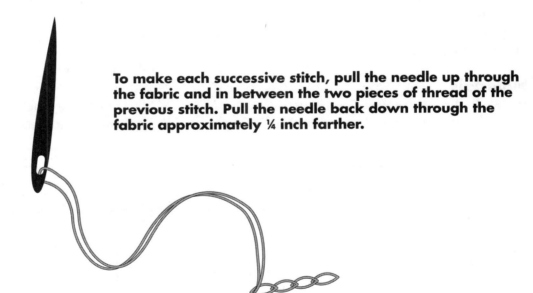

To make each successive stitch, pull the needle up through the fabric and in between the two pieces of thread of the previous stitch. Pull the needle back down through the fabric approximately ¼ inch farther.

Weave a Puppy Place Mat

Here's an activity that will make mealtime more of an elegant dining experience for your dog. If you like how the finished mat looks, you can make some for you and your family to use on the dinner table, too.

Materials
* 1 8½-by-11-inch piece of construction paper (If you use 9-by-12-inch sheets, you'll have to trim 1 inch off the length to fit the finished place mat into the plastic bag.)
* Pencil
* Ruler
* Scissors
* Old magazines
* Stickers
* Markers or crayons
* 1-gallon zip-top plastic freezer bag

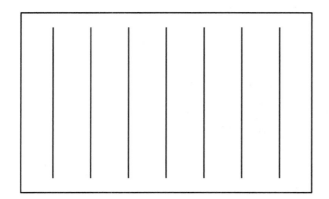

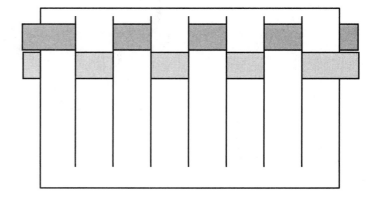

Directions

Draw vertical lines on a piece of construction paper, one inch apart and one inch from the top and bottom (horizontal) edges of the paper. Gently poke the scissors through the paper at the beginning of each line, and cut to the end of the line. Look through the magazines for brightly colored pages, and cut these pages lengthwise into strips measuring ½- to 1½-inches wide. Cut 8 to 12 strips each from a different magazine page. One at a time, weave these cut strips of paper on to the construction paper in an alternating over-and-under pattern: thread the first magazine strip over the first construction paper strip and then under the second, and so on until the magazine strip is woven all the way across the construction paper. Push this first magazine strip down to the bottommost part of the construction paper. Weave the second magazine strip into the construction paper using the opposite pattern that you used for the first strip. Push this one down to the top of the first strip. Continue weaving strips until the construction paper strips are filled. Decorate the mat with colorful stickers and markers. When you've finished decorating the place mat, slip it into the zip-top plastic freezer bag and seal. Place it under your dog's food dish, and ring the dinner bell. Once a week wipe off the plastic bag with a wet towel and flip it over for a different colorful place mat.

 Paws for Thought

The first dog show was held in England in 1859.

Make a Wall Hanging Collage

You can give your puppy or dog a treat for his eyes as well as his belly by hanging a collage in front of his food and water bowls.

Materials
* Old magazines or pet-store advertisements
* Scissors
* Construction paper
* Glue
* Magnet or masking tape
* 1 gallon zip-top plastic freezer bag

Directions
Look through old magazines and cut out pictures of any dogs or puppies you see. Look for pictures of things your dog loves to play with, like a bone, ball, stick, Frisbee, and you, and cut these out, too. Glue these cutout pictures to a piece of construction paper in all different directions, such as right-side up, upside down, and facing left, diagonal, or right until you have the entire piece of paper covered. Once the paper is completely covered, turn it over and cut off the edges of any picture that is hanging over the edge of the paper. Use masking tape to hang the collage on the wall, or, if your dog's bowls are in front of an appliance such as a washing machine, use a magnet to hang the collage. Does the collage help improve your dog's table manners?

If you want to make this collage a place mat, place it inside a sealed zip-top plastic freezer bag. This will help keep your picture dry in case your dog is a sloppy eater!

Option: If you have trouble finding pictures in magazines, ask an adult if you can make a collage out of some old photographs of your pet, maybe even pictures of your pet with family members or friends.

Want to take your dog on your next vacation? You're not alone. A recent Gallup poll showed that 34 percent of dog owners vacation with their animals. But many dogs get carsick. You can try to avoid this messy problem if you prepare your dog for an up-coming road trip. If you make your dog familiar and comfortable with being inside the car, he will be less likely to get sick when you're on a long road trip. By doing these exercises, you'll also help eliminate the anxiety your dog may get if the only time he's in the car is when you're taking him to the veterinarian.

Words of caution before you begin: Never do these exercises just after your dog has eaten. Also, make sure that your dog goes to the bath-room just before or close to the time you begin these exercises.

1. Take him out to the car and sit with him for a while. Let him explore, sniff, and become familiar with the smells and objects in the car.

2. Do this a few times without ever going anywhere.

3. Ask an adult to drive you and your dog on a short trip around the block. Do this a few times before you take him on the road, and everyone will have a more comfortable ride.

Remember to pack all the things your dog needs to make him comfortable on a road trip, including his food and water supplies plus treats, toys, and his bed. Also take a leash and plastic bags to pick up after your dog. When you're on the road and you come to a rest stop, *before* you open the car door make sure your dog is on his leash, because he could get excited from the new surroundings and bolt.

Here are some tips to make your road trip safe as well as fun.

- Take a copy of your dog's vaccination records with you.

- Call your destinations ahead of time and make sure they allow pets. (See Appendix 2 for books that provide long lists of hotels, motels, and inns that allow pets.)

- Take a picture of your dog. Accidents can happen, and if you forget to leash your dog before opening the car door or if she gets loose when you take her for a walk, having a picture to show others will help you find her.

- Have a special dog tag made that lists the name of the dog and a relative, neighbor, or friend's phone number. If your dog gets loose and someone finds her, they'll have someone to call to report the found dog.

- Always place your dog in a carrier in the car. Like a seat belt, this will help restrain her and will make sure she doesn't startle the driver.

 Dog Days of Summer

Early July to mid-August are often referred to as dog days because they are the hottest days of the year in the Northern Hemisphere. Originally these were the days when Sirius, the Dog Star, rose just before or at about the same time as sunrise. (This is no longer true.) Some ancient civilizations believed that Sirius was the cause of the hot, sultry weather; hence, the name dog days.

Design a Howdy Hat

This activity shows you how to make a hat for your dog. This hat should rest on top of your dog's head and between her ears. If you like how it looks, you can make one for yourself.

Materials

* 1 plastic or Styrofoam container from a grocery store deli counter, bottom only
* 1 piece of cardboard
* Pencil
* Ruler
* Scissors
* 3 12-inch pieces of ribbon or yarn
* Clear plastic tape
* Acrylic paint
* Paintbrushes
* Crayons or markers

Directions

Place the plastic container upside down on the center of the piece of cardboard. Trace around the outside of the widest end of the container. Use the ruler to measure ¼-inch all around the inside of the circle you just traced. Draw a second circle using these marks. Cut the smaller circle out.

Use the ruler to measure two inches wider than the bowl circle, and draw a third circle all the way around. Cut around the outside of this circle. Now you have a large cardboard donut that you can place over your plastic container. Because you drew and cut out a smaller circle than the widest end of the bowl, when you place the donut over the smaller end of the container, the cardboard donut should tightly fit.

Use the pencil point to make two holes in the cardboard on opposite sides of the plastic container about one-half inch away from it. Pull one piece of ribbon (or yarn) through one hole and knot the top of it so the ribbon will not go all the way through. Pull another piece of ribbon through the other hole and knot this, too. Tape the last piece of ribbon around the plastic container where it meets the cardboard brim.

Use paints, crayons, or markers to decorate the hat—maybe even paint the name of your dog on the hat. You can paint it with a western theme and draw cacti and mountains on the brim, and, when this dries, you can continue the pattern on the underside. Maybe paint a setting sun on the container. You can do the Tie on a Bandanna activity (see page 35) to complete this cowdog theme.

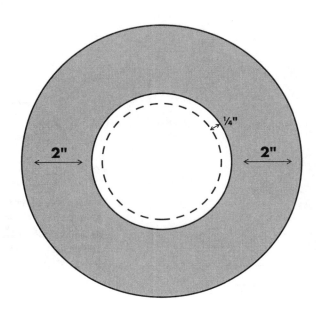

Trace the widest rim of the bowl in the center of the cardboard ring. Measure ¼ inch in and cut out this smaller circle so the hat brim will rest on the bowl.

Here are some other ideas for decorating the hat.
- Gypsy dog hat
- Princess or prince dog hat
- Party dog hat (Place tiny drops of glue all over the hat, then shake some glitter on top of it. The glitter will stick wherever you have glue.)
- Space dog helmet
- Safari dog hat
- Circus dog hat
- Fiesta dog hat (Glue colored balls of cotton all the way around the bottom of the outer edge of the brim.)

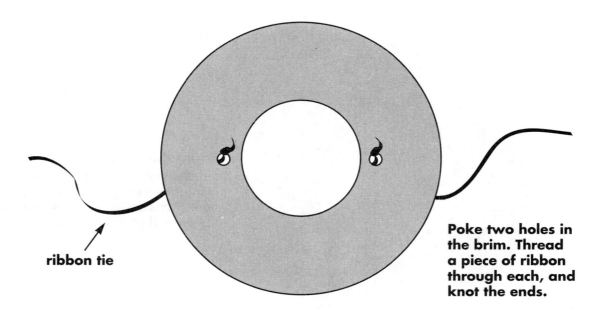

ribbon tie

Poke two holes in the brim. Thread a piece of ribbon through each, and knot the ends.

34

Tie on a Bandanna

Depending on the size of your dog, select a piece of fabric that is large enough to comfortably tie around his neck and look cool, but not so long that he'll trip over it.

Materials

✳ Handkerchief or square-shaped napkin (Note: A traditional bandanna measures 21 by 21 inches. If you select an already cut piece of fabric, you won't have to sew the edges to prevent fraying. Of course, if you're keeping with the cowdog theme of the Howdy Hat activity, then frayed edges might be just what you want.)

✳ Newspapers

✳ Permanent markers

✳ Rubber stamps

✳ Nontoxic ink pad

Directions

Spread newspapers out on a tabletop and place the fabric on top of them. Use markers to decorate the bandanna any way you want. A traditional bandanna uses two colors—usually black and white—and has circular swirls and dot patterns around the edges with little decoration on the interior. If you don't want to draw a pattern, you can draw a picture of you and your dog, with your dog doing an activity he enjoys in his favorite place, or your whole family. Use the rubber stamps to add another decorative element.

Let the fabric dry overnight. To tie the bandanna onto your dog, fold the fabric diagonally so that you change the square shape into a triangle. If you have a medium or large dog, you can tie the bandanna around his neck. Make sure that when you tie it, you can fit two fingers between the fabric and your dog's neck so that the bandanna will be comfortable.

The bandanna should be worn in addition to your dog's collar, which holds his identification and vaccination tags. If you like the way your dog's bandanna looks, make one for yourself, too.

Dog Campers

Some wilderness areas allow you to take a pet with proper identification and a leash. You can buy a pack especially made for a dog so he can carry his own camping equipment, such as food, a bowl for food and one for water, rawhide bones, treats, a favorite toy or two, and maybe even some water. These packs rest on the animal's back and fasten underneath. Be careful not to overload your dog. Take his physical condition and size into consideration before filling his pack.

Be sure to take frequent food and water breaks for both you and your dog to maintain a good energy level. At night, keep your dog with you in your tent so that he won't get lost or have a close encounter with a creature from the wild.

Spend a little time preparing for your camping adventure by helping your dog brush up on obedience training so that you don't end up chasing him through the woods after his first squirrel sighting.

 ## Sunlight Is Good for Dogs

Sunlight destroys bacteria and is a dog's main source of vitamins A and D. So in the winter when the sun is shining, bundle up and take a stroll around the block. It's good for you both.

3

Safety First

It's important to keep your home a safe place for your dog. Even when you're not home, establishing a few simple rules will help you keep your dog safe and happy 24 hours a day.

Make Your Home a Safe Doghouse

Making your home safe for a dog is similar to making your home safe for a baby. Here are some tips.

- Don't leave cleaners out.

- Keep all batteries in a drawer that your pet can't open.

- Make sure there are no wires or cords that a dog can get tangled in or chew on.

- Put plastic electrical outlet covers over unused outlets.

- Unplug appliances when not in use.

- Tie up all electrical cords and try to keep them out of your dog's reach. If this isn't possible, try rubbing a bit of cayenne pepper on the cords, or buy a pet repellent spray.

- Keep plastic grocery bags out of reach. (A sugarlike substance is used to keep the bags from sticking together, and dogs and cats are attracted to this.)

- Be careful when you open the door to go outside. Look to see if your dog is close by. Does your door open into a hallway or porch, or is the street just a quick leap away?

- Keep all toilet-seat lids down. This water is not clean to drink, and a curious animal can be injured when trying to see what's inside this open bowl.

- Hang up your clothes and put away your shoes. Your dog can choke on something as small as a button or as thin as a shoelace.

- Don't leave toys around that are small enough to fit in your dog's mouth.

40

- Put away all your school supplies and little shiny things like paper clips and thumbtacks.

- Keep medicine out of reach.

- Make sure all sewing supplies are put away and out of reach.

- Provide good training to help you and your dog get along better.

- Throw out the garbage regularly. Smelly garbage is a magnet for pets. Keep all your garbage out of reach, either covered or in a kitchen cabinet.

- Some animals learn how to open cabinets. If your dog learns this trick, baby-proof your cabinets with plastic hooks or other devices.

- Don't leave any chocolate out! Chocolate can be lethal to dogs and cats. Semisweet dark chocolate, especially cooking chocolate, is the worst. How much they eat and the size of your dog makes a difference to how dangerous it is. If you think your dog has eaten chocolate, call your veterinarian immediately.

- If your dog gets into anything with alkaline in it, such as a drain cleaner, *The Doctors Book of Home Remedies for Dogs and Cats* suggests giving him three teaspoons of vinegar or lemon juice diluted with three teaspoons of water. Ingested poison can also be absorbed by activated charcoal. This comes in a tablet or powder form that should be mixed with water. But both of these are temporary fixes. Get your dog to your veterinarian immediately for a more permanent solution. In either case, do *not* try to get your dog to vomit!

Can you think of other ways to make your home a safe doghouse?

Decorate a Collar

There are different types of dog collars available. Here are two that are very animal friendly. The first is the traditional neck collar that is made of woven nylon or leather. The second type is the harness collar. This fits around your dog's chest and prevents your dog from choking if he's more eager to move forward than you are. The harness collar is the most comfortable for the dog, but because she'll be able to use the full power of her body, your dog will be more likely to pull you along with her . . . at her pace. Ready, set, run!

You can make a decorative collar for your dog and one for you, too.

Materials
* 2 nylon or leather collars
* 2 heavy books
* Craft glue
* Colorful rhinestones, available at craft or art supply stores
* Permanent markers
* Yarn
* Scissors
* Colorful beads

 Play It Safe

Don't string any beads to your dog's collar, because he might try to eat the beads and could choke.

Directions

Place both collars right side up on top of a table, and place heavy books at each end to secure the collars while you work. Glue the rhinestones to the collars, and use the markers to color the collars in between the rhinestones. Let this dry completely. While the glue is drying, you can create something else to add to your collar (not your dog's). Cut yarn into two- to four-inch pieces. String one bead on each piece of yarn. When the rhinestones have dried completely, wrap a cut piece of yarn with a bead attached around your collar and knot it. Tie each piece of beaded string loosely enough around the collar so that it hangs down. If you use different lengths of yarn, your beads will hang at different lengths.

When completely dry, put the collar around your dog's neck next to the one that holds his license, identification, and vaccination tags. Now he's stylin' and safe.

A Proper Fit

A proper fit for a neck collar is when hooked, it is loose enough to fit two fingers between the collar and your dog's body. This amount of looseness will allow your dog to breathe without difficulty.

Choosing a Veterinarian

hoosing a veterinarian is the most important decision you'll have to make after you've picked out your beloved four-legged friend. When you take your adult dog (older than one year) to the veterinarian for his yearly checkup and booster shots, or if he's having a problem, the veterinarian can tell you the general condition of your dog, but only with your help. You'll need to tell her how your dog is doing and, if he's ill,

describe his symptoms. Because you're a big part of maintaining the good health of your dog, your veterinarian should be someone you feel comfortable with—someone who you can talk to and ask questions and someone who takes time with both you and your dog. Also when you're shopping for a veterinarian, be sure to ask the doctor if she or the clinic offers emergency service at night or on the weekend.

 Yummy Ways to Disguise Pills

It can be tough to get your dog to take a pill whether he's sick and needs pills to feel better or as a regular supplement. Placing a pill in the middle of a ball of one of these tasty treats will help the medicine go down.

- Cream cheese
- Liverwurst
- Peanut butter
- Soft dog treat

Going to the veterinarian is part of dog owner-ship. Just as it's important to take your puppy to the veterinarian many times in her first year of life, yearly visits and vaccinations are essential, too. This activity will help you keep track of your dog's shots. Like a progress report or report card from school, this activity will tell you what your dog's been up to.

Materials
* Plain white paper
* Dog vaccination chart (next page)
* Pencil
* Markers
* Magnet

 ## Heartworm Disease: Prevention Is the Best Medicine

Heartworm disease is a very serious condition for dogs. Carried by mosquitoes, heartworms, which are long spaghetti-like worms, can grow and live inside your dog's heart chambers and major blood vessels. These worms make it increasingly difficult for your dog to breathe because as the worms grow, they make it more difficult for blood to flow freely. While heartworm-carrying mosquitoes are especially common in the southeast, there is no place without risk because mosquitoes are everywhere.

The easiest way to treat heartworms is before they start. Your veterinarian must test your dog first before prescribing heartworm preventive medicine. This can be a chewable or liquid medication that is given to your dog daily or monthly depending on her outside activity level and where you live.

Place the white paper over the dog vaccination chart and trace the outline of it. Next, write the words on this chart in the proper places. Your chart should have two columns for every year, one for the date the vaccination is due and one for the date of the actual vaccination. Calculate and write the date when your dog's next shot is due using the number of months listed on the dog vaccination chart. Use markers to decorate this chart with all kinds of things that your dog likes to play with, like a bone, a ball, or you. Draw a column for every year so that you can keep this chart for a long time. Use a magnet to hang this on the refrigerator.

DOG VACCINATION CHART

Disease	Revaccination Intervals								
	1999			2000			2001		
	In Months	Date Due	Actual Date	In Months	Date Due	Actual Date	In Months	Date Due	Actual Date
Distemper*	12			12			12		
Infectious canine hepatitis* (CAV-1 or CAV-2)	12			12			12		
Parvovirus infection*	12			12			12		
Bordetella* (kennel cough)	12			12			12		
Parainfluenza* (kennel cough)	12			12			12		
Leptospirosis*	12			12			12		
Rabies	12 or 36**			12 or 36			12 or 36		
Coronavirus*	12			12			12		

*Can be combined in one shot
**Check with your veterinarian as to the type of vaccine

If you have more than one dog in your home, it's important to give them all the same vaccination protection. You can do this by getting all your animals vaccinated at the same time. You can vaccinate some of your dogs early to match the dates of your newer dog. Then all future vaccinations will be due at the same time. This will make it easier to remember each animal's vaccination history and provides each animal with the same protection at all times.

 Ways to Make a Trip to the Veterinarian Less Stressful

- Take your dog on short car trips (but never leave her alone in the car), so she learns that getting in the car doesn't always mean she's going to the veterinarian.

- Stop in and say hello to your veterinarian without having an examination. This will help your dog get familiar with the veterinarian without fearing him.

- When you are there for an appointment, ask your veterinarian to approach your dog on his knees or while sitting on the ground so that he's seeing eye to eye with your pal.

- Bring treats along for your veterinarian to give to your dog during the examination.

- Offer your dog a treat when your veterinarian is ready to give him a shot. This will help distract your dog from the pain.

- Have a conversation with the veterinarian so the dog learns that you are OK with being there and that the veterinarian respects you.

- You can ask your veterinarian to do these things to help ease your dog's anxiety, but a good vet will already do these and will probably have a few more tricks up her sleeve.

Time to Brush Everyone's Teeth

Giving your dog rawhide treats will take care of his urge to chew. But did you know that these treats also help scrape off plaque and tartar that build up on his teeth? If you give your dog rawhide treats and his breath still stinks, try a natural breath freshener like raw, minced carrots, parsley, or mint. If these don't work, maybe it's time to brush his teeth.

One of the easiest ways to get your dog to let you brush his teeth is to start when he's a puppy. If it's part of his regular grooming routine, he'll accept it much easier as he ages.

This activity requires an adult partner. It's essential that an adult do the brushing while you read the directions and perform the important cheerleading duties. Never try to brush your dog's teeth on your own.

Here are the warm-up steps. First, stroke the outside of you dog's cheeks with your fingers. Do this twice a day for a week. Second, start out with a finger toothbrush. This will help your pet become accustomed to having your hands around his mouth. A finger toothbrush has short, rubber bristles on one side of the fingertip pad.

(For puppies and smaller dogs, this might be the only toothbrush you'll need; just add the toothpaste as suggested here.) Third, introduce your dog to toothpaste made especially for dogs. The paste has delicious flavors like chicken, beef, or peanut butter—yum out! (*Never* use people toothpaste.) Let your dog lick the paste off your finger. Do this for a couple of days and still stroke the outside of his cheeks. Fourth, place a small amount of the toothpaste on the toothbrush and let him lick it off the brush.

Now that this gradual introduction to toothbrushing is complete, you and your toothbrushing partner are ready to begin. Gently pull back your dog's lips and cheeks and begin brushing with short, back-and-forth strokes at the gumline. This is where tartar and plaque are most likely to form. Brush only a few teeth the first time, and add a few more teeth each time.

Here's your VIP role. Because your dog will not be comfortable with this type of attention at first, it's very important for you to be the cheerleader—give him a lot of reassurance during these steps, and praise him when he behaves. You can give him a little treat after each session, such as a small dog biscuit or a new rawhide—

 The Goodness of Garlic

Dog breath can be a real problem, so why do some experts suggest giving him garlic? The goodness of garlic is that the odor will penetrate his coat and make it less tasty to fleas. Garlic can also be used as a weight-loss tool by helping the liver and gallbladder (important digestive organs) work better.

Convinced? If so, how much garlic should you feed your dog? The recommended dosage for small dogs is one-fourth to one-half of one clove each day; for larger dogs, feed them one to two cloves each day.

both good helpers in the war against plaque and gum disease. Eventually, if you work as a team, brushing your dog's teeth will become a comfortable part of your dog-care routine.

Another thing you can do is buy a toy for your dog that helps clean her teeth.

Bad doggy breath can be a sign of a more serious condition, such as a digestive problem or mouth infection. If, after brushing your dog's teeth, the odor continues, call your veterinarian.

Leave Your Dog at Home

Don't leave your dog alone in the car, especially on a warm day (70° or more). The inside of a car will quickly get dangerously hot: in less than 10 minutes, the temperature inside your car can reach 102° or more, and in 30 minutes, it can get up to 120° degrees or more.

Also, a dog left unattended in a car can be easily stolen.

Here are some signs of heatstroke from The Anti-Cruelty Society:
- Difficulty in breathing, then sudden rapid breathing
- Abnormally red gums and tongue
- A blank or anxious stare
- Disorientation or sudden collapse

If you think your pet is overheated, immediately immerse, cover, or rub your dog with cool (not cold or ice) water to lower his body temperature. When the excessive panting subsides, take him to a veterinarian for an emergency examination. Even if it seems your dog has recovered, a vet should check him for any internal damage.

Prevention is one of the best ways to keep your dog cool and happy. So don't leave him in the car; leave him at home.

Bath Time

The best way to teach your dog to enjoy or at least tolerate being bathed is to start bathing her regularly when she's young. (Get a helping hand from a parent or older sibling.) You should bathe your dog as needed and especially after she discovers the joys of playing in the mud or starts to smell bad. In general, if you bathe your dog more than once each month, you can give her dry skin. (You can try to use this same argument with a parent, but there's no guarantee it'll work.)

Use a mild dog shampoo or baby shampoo. You can also use a rinse that is designed to repel fleas. Many of these have nice soft fragrances. Be careful not to get the shampoo in her eyes. When you're finished, thoroughly towel dry her and maybe even use a blow dryer, constantly moving it over her body. When using a blow dryer, a nice treat in wintertime, always keep your hand on the area you're drying to be aware of how hot it is on your dog.

Materials
* Bristle brush
* Water
* Mild dog shampoo, baby shampoo, or a rinse for dogs that contains a mild flea repellent
* Comb
* Towel
* Blow dryer

Directions
To wash your dog, a bristle brush that's a mix of nylon (very hard) and natural (soft) bristles is best. First get your dog wet and make sure her coat is completely soaked. Then put a little bit of shampoo on her back and use your hands to massage the shampoo into her coat. Gently brush your dog's fur. Shampoo her legs, tail, belly, head, neck, chest, and the outside of her ears. Be careful to keep the shampoo out of her eyes and ears. Washing her the same way every time will help her learn what to expect.

Combing your dog is a good way to get rid of mats or prevent them from occurring. The comb you use will depend on your dog's coat.

Type of Comb	Type of Hair
Fine-tooth	Soft, silky, or short hair (such as an Irish setter or terrier)
Medium-tooth	Average coat texture (such as a Labrador retriever)
Wide-tooth	Dense or heavy coat (such as a sheepdog)

When you're finished washing and drying with a towel and a blow dryer, wash the used comb and/or brush in warm, soapy water. It's also a good idea to occasionally wash her collar and leash.

 ## I Smell a Skunk

If you take your dog for a walk and he gets sprayed by a skunk, or if you start to let your dog in the house one day and you notice he smells like a skunk—it's an unmistakable aroma— here are a few tips to clean up the air and your pet.

• If possible, bathe him outdoors. Tomato juice poured over his coat will help absorb the odor. Repeat this tomato juice bathing process at least twice.

• Throw away his collar (after removing his tags), leash, and anything else that was on his body when he was sprayed by the skunk. If the skunk sprayed him while you were walking your dog, it is a good idea to throw away all your clothes, too. Hopefully you weren't in the direct line of fire, so a tomato juice bath for you shouldn't be necessary.

The best way to teach your dog to enjoy being brushed is to start when she's young. Regular brushing stimulates your dog's skin and helps her produce natural oils that help protect her coat. Also, parasites like fleas, lice, and ticks hate to be disturbed. Grooming your dog daily to loosen her hair will prevent mats and harass these little critters.

Here are some tips to a good grooming session.

- Begin grooming early! Start grooming your dog when she's a puppy. Grooming early and often will help her get used to this kind of handling and will make this regular event a lot easier on you both.

- Talk to her as you groom her. This will help her feel comfortable.

- Always brush her the same way every time so she'll learn what to expect. If you started with her back last time and then brushed each of her legs, make it a habit to brush her in the same order next time.

- Begin and end by brushing her back. She'll like this a lot, and if she doesn't like you brushing her ears, for example, she'll sit still for it as long as she knows that you'll brush her back again before you finish.

- Brush in the same direction as the hair grows. If your dog has long hair that hangs off her body (like an Irish setter or an Afghan), brush in a downward motion toward the floor.

What Kind of Brush Do I Use?

For most coats, a wire slicker brush is all that you will need for regular grooming. However, you can get a second brush that is designed for your dog's particular type of coat. To select a good second brush to use on your dog, look at his coat. Does your dog have a smooth coat with short hair like a bulldog, Labrador retriever, beagle, dachshund, or pug? If so, a rubber curry brush, grooming mitt, or natural-bristle brush is a good tool. If your dog has a long, flowing coat like an Afghan, springer spaniel, Pekingese, shih tzu, or Old English sheepdog, try a steel-tooth rake. If you're not certain, check with your groomer or veterinarian to buy the brush that's best for your dog's coat.

Here are some tips for while you're grooming.

- While brushing, be sure to give your dog a lot of praise and let him know how glad you are that he is behaving.

- Only move your dog's legs in natural positions. Be careful not to pull or twist her legs or raise them too high as you groom.

- If brushing irritates your dog's skin (don't press too hard when brushing), a light dusting of cornstarch baby powder will bring relief.

Whenever grooming your dog, getting a helping hand from an adult is a good idea. This way you can trade off brushing and praising your dog.

wire slicker brush　　**steel-tooth rake**

Play Beauty Shop

You can make your dog beautiful for a special occasion. You don't have to sew a complicated outfit or spend a lot of money on doggie clothes for holidays and parties. All you need are a few trimmings and a little time to make your dog look extra special. Always have an adult help you with this because you will be grooming your dog in new, unfamiliar ways, and you want her to feel comfortable. Remember to praise her a lot if she behaves while grooming her.

Make a Mohawk
Here's a fun way to style your dog's hair.

Materials
* Comb
* Small hair clips
* Water-based hair gel

Directions

You must have a longhaired dog to make a mohawk. To make a mohawk, comb your dog's hair first. Separate the hair that you want to put in a mohawk by making parts in your dog's coat and then back-combing the hair. Use a hair clip to secure this hair. Put a small amount of water-based hair gel in your hands, and, when you're ready, have your partner remove the clip while you grab the hair that will fall out. Press this hair together using the palms of your hands. Work from the base of the hair to the top, slowly moving up and squishing your dog's hair between your hands. Continue with this motion or apply more gel if necessary until this hair stands up on its own. (Note: Giving your dog a bath soon after this activity is a good idea. See the Bath Time activity earlier in this chapter.)

Help Your Dog See the Light of Day

Does your dog have long hair that often flops down in front of her eyes? You can help her see by making a little waterfall on top of her head.

Materials

✳ Comb
✳ Elastic hair band
✳ Ribbon

Comb the hair on top of your dog's head. With your hands, gather the hair on top of her head and hold it. Use an elastic hair band to tie this hair together at the base of her head, wrapping the hair band around the hair a few times—enough so that it will hold the hair, but not so tight that it will pull your dog's hair.

You can add an extra splash to this look by adding a colorful ribbon tied in a bow on top of the elastic band.

For Beautiful, Shorthaired Dogs

If your dog has a shorthaired coat, you can still make her beautiful by tying different colorful ribbons around her neck. If you cut three different colored ribbons, you can make a bright braided necklace for her. If your dog is tall enough, add a pendant to this necklace by cutting out a piece of cardboard in the shape of a heart, poking a hole in it, and threading the braided ribbon through it. Loosely tie this necklace around your dog's neck. (This necklace should not replace, but be an addition to, your dog's collar with her identification, license, and vaccination tags on it.)

Nonchemical Pest Control

Here are some chemical-free ways to eliminate pesky pests such as ticks and fleas.

- Immature ticks wait in low vegetation, so keep your grass cut short. Ask an adult to trim any hedges so low branches, which your dog can reach, are eliminated.

- If you have an outside dog run or pen, trim the tall grass around it. Don't use hay or straw for bedding, because this can be tick infested.

- If your family is going to plant sod in the yard, buy a brand that is guaranteed to be tickfree.

- Wash your dog's bedding in hot water at least once a week. Hot water kills fleas, lice, and ticks that may be present.

- Feed your dog a little bit of garlic (see sidebar earlier in this chapter), or sprinkle some dry yeast occasionally on his food. These additions work to eliminate fleas from the inside out.

 Hot Stuff

Sprinkling cayenne pepper on an ant trail can help get rid of these little pests without hurting your dog. If the smell of the pepper doesn't prevent your dog from licking the cayenne pepper, tasting it once will be enough. She won't do it again, and it won't hurt her like some bug sprays.

- Bathe your dog. First try a nonmedicated pet shampoo. If he continues to scratch, bathe him again using a flea shampoo.

- Vacuum your carpets daily during flea season.

- Add 6 to 10 mothballs to the vacuum cleaner bag before sealing it and throwing it away.

- The scent of fruits and leaves such as lemon, eucalyptus, and peppermint will repel insects. Rubbing these scents on a pet collar works for repelling fleas for both dogs and cats.

- Comb your dog daily. Special closely spaced tooth combs will help remove fleas. These combs are available from your vet or in local pet-supply stores. Kill any fleas pulled out by frequently dipping the comb in very warm soapy water while grooming.

- Ask an adult for help if you find any ticks stuck into the skin of your dog. An adult can use a pair of tweezers to carefully remove the tick, including its head, which is frequently buried beneath the skin. For stubborn ticks, smear a little petroleum jelly on top of the tick to smother it. Wait several minutes. The tick will either pull out of the skin because it is suffocating, or it will die and become limp. Then an adult can use tweezers with a fine point to carefully pull off the *entire* tick. Once the tick is removed, wash this area with soap and water. If the tick's head remains imbedded in the skin, see your veterinarian. Ticks can carry very serious diseases, such as Rocky Mountain spotted fever and Lyme disease. Wash your hands carefully after removing fleas or ticks from your dog, because they can be harmful to you, too.

- Pick up and throw away dog droppings in your yard at least once a day.

- Mineral oil will kill ear mites. Have an adult use an eyedropper to place a few drops of this oil in each ear, massage, wait about five minutes, and then remove the oil with cotton balls or swabs.

- Fleas dislike some herbs, including rosemary, santolina, chamomile, southernwood, wormwood, celery, and parsley. You can weave these herbs on a collar or sprinkle them in your dog's bed and add fresh herbs on a weekly basis.

If you still need help, make an appointment to see your vet.

Get Your Dog Hooked!

ere's a great way to always be able to locate your dog-walking supplies, such as your dog's leash, plastic bags to clean up after your dog, your house keys, a Frisbee, or whatever else you like to take on walks.

Materials

✻ Pencil
✻ 1 10-by-14-inch piece of cardboard, or larger
✻ Ruler
✻ Scissors
✻ 1 12-by-15-inch piece of fabric, or at least larger than the piece of cardboard
✻ Craft glue
✻ 3 plastic self-adhesive hooks
✻ Glitter, stickers, colorful beads, or feathers
✻ 2 nails
✻ Hammer
(Adult help is suggested.)

Directions

Draw the face of a dog, a dog paw, or a bone on the piece of cardboard. Draw the picture so that it is at least 14 inches across and 7 inches tall. Cut the picture out. (Ask an adult to help you if the cardboard is thick and difficult to cut.) Place your cardboard image on top of the back of the fabric.

Winter Walking Tip

When you take your dog for a walk in the snow, ice and salt can injure her paw pads. Once you return home from your walk, use a damp cloth to wipe off any ice or salt residue from her pads. Also be sure to dry her completely.

Trace around this and cut it out. Use craft glue to glue the fabric to the cardboard. Before peeling, place the three hooks on your cloth-covered cardboard and use a pencil to mark where you'd like to place them. Peel off the paper tape back from each hook, and place it on the marked spot. Push down firmly to secure. Use glitter, stickers, colorful beads, or feathers to decorate.

A good place to hang this is near the door you exit from when taking your dog for a walk. Check with an adult first, and get his or her help with the hammering. Place the nails far enough apart so they will support your art and angled so they will not rip through the cardboard. Hammer the nails into the wall.

 Be Kind to Your Dog's Paws in Winter

Most dogs and cats can't endure extremely cold weather for more than 10 to 15 minutes even though they have fur coats. As a general rule, if it's too cold for you to be outside, it's probably too cold for your dog to be outside, too. An animal left outdoors can get frostbite. Frostbite signs include skin that is cool to the touch and a decreased sensation in that area. If you think your dog may have frostbite, gently thaw the area with a towel soaked in warm water and then take your dog to the veterinarian immediately. If frostbite has occurred, this area will become red and painful and in the future will more easily become frostbitten.

Create a Safety Board

There are so many things to remember in an emergency. If your dog gets injured you're going to be upset and want help immediately. This activity will help you prepare for the unexpected. Keep this safety board near the phone that you use most. Always keep this board in the same place, and make sure everyone in your household knows where it's kept.

Materials
✳ Notebook paper
✳ Pen
✳ 1-gallon zip-top plastic freezer bag
✳ Magnet or masking tape

Directions
Collect the following information to include on your safety board:

Emergency Resources
- ASPCA National Animal Poison Control Center (800) 548-2423 (Remember that this number requires a credit card number when you call.)
- Veterinarian's name and phone number
- Veterinarian's office address and directions
- Veterinarian's home phone number
- Phone number of and directions to the closest 24-hour emergency animal hospital

Your Information
- Name
- Home address
- Home phone number
- School name, address, and phone number
- Name and phone number of a neighbor
- Name and phone number of your nearest-living relative

Your Dog's Information

- Dog's name
- Dog's date of birth
- Dog's breed
- A recent picture of your dog
- Attach a copy of your Vaccination Chart (See Chapter 1 for the puppy chart or earlier in this chapter for the adult dog chart.)
- Attach a photocopy of your dog's current license
- List your dog's current medications
- List your dog's allergies

Slip these pages into a zip-top plastic freezer bag (to protect it from smears or smudges), and use the magnet or masking tape to keep this right next to the phone. Update this once a year or whenever you return home from a visit to the veterinarian. This might take a little time and a bit of effort to complete, but in an emergency, you'll be glad you did. If you have to run to your veterinarian or local animal hospital for emergency care, take this list with you. Also, if you think your dog has eaten something that is making him sick, take along whatever substance your dog has ingested or eaten, whether it's a food item, medicine, or a toxic substance. Remember, minutes are precious in an emergency.

Be Kind to Your Dog's Ears

Dogs have very sensitive hearing, and loud noises are *extremely* loud and frightening to them. Never scream around your dog. Dogs can react in a number of ways, including hiding under furniture, snapping, or even biting. If you scream a lot, over time your dog will try to avoid you so he can get away from the source of the loud noise.

Just like you, sometimes your dog gets hurt. It's a good idea to get an adult's help immediately, and, in severe cases, take your dog to the veterinarian as soon as possible. Here are some emergency supplies to help keep your dog comfortable until you can get him medical attention. (See Appendix 2 for helpful books and important phone numbers for use in an emergency.)

In one large box or two plastic bins that close, store the following items:

Emergency Care Supplies
* Crate, large enough to fit your dog comfortably for a short ride to the veterinarian
* Extra collar
* Extra leash
* Copy of dog license
* Copy of vaccination chart (See activity in this chapter for dogs or Chapter 1 for puppies.)

* List of medications
* Flame-retardant blanket
* Charcoal tablets (When mixed with water, these can absorb poisons until you can get your dog to the veterinarian or an emergency clinic.)
* Bottled water
* 1 package pet treats, unopened
* Roll of adhesive bandages
* 2-inch gauze bandages
* Antibiotic ointment or cortisone skin ointment
* Antibiotic eye ointment
* Eye wash
* Flea powder
* Flea rinse
* Gauze
* Tape
* Hydrogen peroxide
* Scissors
* Zinc cream

* Aspirin
* Nail clippers (Ask your veterinarian about the proper type for your dog.)
* Rubbing alcohol
* Tweezers
* Rectal thermometer
* Petroleum jelly
* Towel
* Squirt bottle filled with water
* Small bottle of soapy water to clean wounds
* Any medications your dog is currently taking
* Pad of paper and pen (to write down injury notes from witnesses or details about poison or substance swallowed)

* 1 copy of *Pet First Aid* book, a helpful guide written by the American Red Cross and the Humane Society of the United States (See Appendix 2 for ordering information.)
* 1 copy of your safety board (See previous activity.)

If your dog is in an emergency, call your veterinarian or the hospital ahead of time to tell them the problem and let them know you're on your way. If it's important that you leave right away, have another family member or friend call and provide this information. If your dog is injured, his instinct is to lick his wound. This is OK and may help in the healing process, so you don't have to stop him.

 ## How to Make a Muzzle Out of Gauze

An injured dog might snap or even bite someone she loves or someone who is trying to help. Have an adult make a muzzle out of gauze before trying to transport your dog for medical attention. Cut a two-foot-long piece of gauze, and tie one big loop in it. Slip the loop around your dog's snout, and loosely tighten it over the bridge of her nose. Tie another knot under the snout, and pull the remaining material behind your dog's ears and tie it in a loose bow. This gauze muzzle can be quickly removed and won't interfere with breathing.

In the wild, dogs live in caves. Caves served as natural dens for these pack animals and helped provide them with protection. Today, companion dogs who are left at home alone for long periods of time may develop a fear of large spaces. You can give your dog the protection of a cave and the comfort of a smaller space inside your home with a crate. A crate, such as a dog carrier or a metal cage, should be large enough so he can sit up and move around, but not so large that he can go to the bathroom at one end of it and sit comfortably in the other end. Crates are sometimes used when house-training dogs

(See House-Training Puppies in Chapter 1 for more information.)

Let your dog's crate be his safe place. Never drag him out of his crate or force him to leave it. When you're not using his crate for house training or to separate animals, keep the crate door open at all times. Let your dog go in there when he needs to get away from other family members.

Never use your dog's crate as a place of punishment. Your dog should only have good memories and experiences with his crate.

This is a great warm-weather activity for you and your friends. You can make your dogs smell nice and fresh while making some extra money, too.

Materials (for each person)
Day 1—Before the Dog Wash
* Paper*
* Colorful markers

Day 2—Dog-Wash Day!
* Mild shampoo
* Bucket
* Garden hose (only 1 needed)

* Sponge
* Natural-bristle brush
* Towels

 Play It Safe

Only wash the dogs of friends or relatives with the owner present at all times. Also, only wash one dog at a time, and keep the dog on a leash. Before you agree to wash a dog, check with the owner to make sure that the dog does not bite.

Directions

Day 1—Before the Dog Wash

Get together with a group of friends and plan a dog wash. First decide on a day and the hours that you want to do this. Next, use paper and markers to create flyers that advertise your services. The flyer should say that you're offering a dog wash and specify the hours you're holding it, the location, and the date and any fee you will be charging. If you are just going to wash your friends' dogs, think about washing each in his own back-yard so he will feel more comfortable. Decorate the flyers with a lot of colors to make them eye-catching and hard to refuse. Each friend who has a dog should take a copy of the flyer home.

Day 2—Dog-Wash Day!

Once all your dog-washing friends have arrived (bathing suits are a good idea on dog-wash day), find out how many dog-washing appointments you have, and decide on an order. For each dog, place a small amount of shampoo in each bucket, and then fill the bucket with water from the hose. Get the dog wet first using the hose. Be careful not to squirt the dog in the face or ears with the water. Run your hands all along the dog's body to make sure that his coat is completely soaked.

Wash the dog using the sponge to get the shampoo on him, and then use your hands or the natural-bristle brush to massage the shampoo into his coat. (See the Bath Time activity earlier in this chapter for more information.)

You can take turns holding the dog and talking sweetly to him. Be kind to him. He may become frightened because of all the noise. Make sure a parent will be present in the house in case the dog gets a little jumpy from all the giggling.

Take your time rinsing the dog to make sure all the shampoo is off. Dried shampoo will become itchy and can dry out a dog's skin. If it's chilly outside, completely towel dry the dog so he won't get too cold. After each dog's turn, empty, wash, and rinse every bucket and brush before beginning to wash the next dog. This is a good way to keep your dogs clean . . . at least for a few minutes.

*If you have a computer, most word-processing programs offer different typeface options and borders. You can design your flyer on your computer screen, print out a lot of copies, and then use markers to make the flyers eye-catching.

Help Finding a Lost Dog

A lost dog is a very sad thing, but you can't give up hope. You must act quickly! The first day or two are the most critical when a dog is missing. If driving around the neighborhood with an adult has not helped you locate your dog, go home and start a lost-dog campaign. Call all your friends to come and help.

Materials

✳ Recent clear picture of your dog
✳ Tape
✳ Plain white paper
✳ Pen
✳ Marker
✳ Tape
✳ Telephone book yellow pages

Directions

Find a recent picture of your dog. Tape it to the top of the paper. Take another sheet of paper and write down all the things you want to include in your sign, including the following:

- A brief description of your dog
- Her name
- A phone number that people can call if your dog is spotted
- Reward information (optional)

Once you have your list of information, use the marker and neatly write it on the paper with the picture taped to it. Take it to a photocopy shop and have copies made—enough to cover one-half to one mile from your home. Ask your friends, in pairs, to go from house to house and tape up signs.

Use the telephone book to identify the veterinarians within a 10-mile radius of your home and shelters within 30 miles of your home. Call each and give them the information about the missing dog. Fax them a poster or drop one off. Even if they haven't seen your dog, ask them to post it because they may have a customer who has seen your dog.

 ## Microchip for Chipper

Many shelters now insert microchip identification tags to help people find their lost pets. The chip is the size of a grain of rice and is injected just below the skin between the shoulder blades. It can't move, and your dog won't get an allergic reaction to it. This tiny chip has an identification number on it. When a dog is brought in to a shelter, he is scanned with a special wand to see if he has an ID chip. If the shelter finds a chip, they'll call a toll-free number where they can get the owner's or veterinarian's information—whoever placed the chip.

This is an easy way to get your dog back home safely.

Whether you use a microchip or a collar with current identification tags, be sure to always have some way for your dog to be identified as yours in case he gets loose. Your best chance to get your dog back is with an identification tag.

Here are some missing-pet locator agencies. Check the yellow pages for a company near your home.

Sherlock Bones, Tracer of Missing Pets
1925 Fages Court
Walnut Creek, CA 94595
(800) 942-6637
www.sherlockbones.com/html/menu.html

They'll help create postcards and posters to assist you in your search. Fees vary. Call for current prices.

National Pet Recovery and Registration
704 Greengate Circle
St. Johns, MI 48879
(800) 984-8638
www.petrecovery.com

They offer a registration service, record the circumstances of your dog's disappearance, and write up a detailed description of the animal. They provide many other services for pet recovery. Fees vary. Call for current prices.

4

Nibbles & Treats

Just like you, your dog has special nutritional needs. A healthy diet for your dog combines food given at nearly the same time and same amount every day, plenty of clean, fresh water all the time, occasional treats, and love and attention from you. All of these things will help your pal stay healthy and happy for many years.

What Makes a Healthy Diet

Descended from wolves, dogs are omnivores (eating both animal and vegetable food). Once domesticated, dogs were fed packaged food that combined the same high-protein diet but in a dried or wet processed form.

Many types of dog food are now available. Commercial dog food is nutritionally balanced and varies depending on the age or weight of your dog. On the store shelves you'll find puppy food, adult dog food, reduced-calorie dog food, food for dogs with allergies, organic dog food, and a formula for older dogs. You'll find food labeled "premium" and food called "regular," in both generic and name-brand varieties. How do you know what foods are right for your dog? The best rule of thumb is to ask your veterinarian. Also, check with the breeder or shelter where you found your dog to find out what kind of food she was getting before she joined your family.

Are Vitamins a Good Idea?

Vitamins and minerals are important for you as well as your dog. But do you need to give your dog vitamin supplements? If you buy name-brand dog food, it is specially formulated to meet your dog's nutritional requirements. That's why there is separate puppy food, adult dog food, and dog food for older dogs. But if you're in doubt, talk to your veterinarian. *Never* give your dog human vitamins—our nutritional needs are very different.

Food not only provides your dog with necessary nourishment, but it also promotes growth and provides health benefits. A regular feeding schedule is important for your dog. Feed him once or twice a day and at the same time every day. Some veterinarians recommend that you feed your dog according to his weight—one cup of dry food for every 20 to 25 pounds. If you have a bathroom scale, you can find out how much he weighs if you weigh yourself first, then hold him and weigh yourself again. If your dog is too big for you to hold, ask an adult to do this. Metal or coated ceramic bowls are better to use as food dishes than plastic bowls. It's difficult to clean plastic bowls thoroughly, and bacteria can grow in them.

Materials
* Newspapers
* Ceramic bowl
* 1 cup water
* 2 teaspoons vinegar
* Measuring cup
* Measuring spoons
* Large mixing bowl
* Towel
* Paper
* Pen or pencil
* Water-based enamel paint for ceramics (nontoxic)
* Paintbrushes

Directions
Spread newspapers on a counter or tabletop. Wash your hands and wash the ceramic bowl. Combine the water and vinegar in the large mixing bowl. Place your ceramic bowl inside the mixing bowl, and cover it completely with this solution by splashing it on the bowl with your hands. This will eliminate any grease or other residue on the ceramic bowl before you begin painting. Dry the bowl completely.

Sketch out your design using paper and pen or pencil before you begin. Here are some ideas.

- A picture of your dog
- His name
- The message "feed me" or another message
- A dog bone
- Shooting stars
- Different size circles and squares
- An outdoor scene with grass, trees, and flowers
- A cat
- A picture of you
- A rainbow

Use the paintbrushes to paint the design you've chosen onto the bowl. You can decorate the inside and the outside of the bowl if you like. When the bowl is dry to the touch, carefully place it inside a cold oven, set the temperature to 325°, and bake the bowl for 30 to 45 minutes. (Note: The colors of the enamels may darken as they are baked into the bowl.) Let the bowl cool completely before removing it from the oven. Wash the bowl with warm water and soap, dry it, and fill it with dog food. Does this new bowl improve your dog's table manners?

 Dog Wisdom

Proverbs are sayings that express things that people believe to be true. Here are some proverbs that dogs have had a paw in. Do you know what these mean?

You can't teach an old dog new tricks. • He who lies down with dogs wakes up with fleas.

Every dog has his day. • Let sleeping dogs lie. • Only dogs stare.

Money will buy you a pretty dog, but it won't buy you the wag of his tail.

The dog's kennel is not the place to keep a sausage. • Can you think of others?

Plan a Birthday/Adoption Day Party

There are many ways to celebrate your dog's birthday.

- Give him a special treat.
- Fix him a special meal.
- Make him a new toy.
- Buy him a new bone.
- Sing *Happy Birthday*.
- Take him to a favorite place such as a park.
- Take photographs of you and your pal.

You can also throw a party for your dog. Invite your friends, their parents, and their dogs to your house. (Parents?!!? The parents can come in handy to help keep the dog guests in check, and they can take care of the dogs when you want to play some games with just your friends.)

Here are some games for you and your friends to share.

Play Pin the Tail on the Birthday Dog Poster

This is just like pin the tail on the donkey but with a much cuter target.

Materials
* Dog poster
* Tape
* Construction paper, close to the color of your dog
* Scissors
* Pen
* Bandanna

Directions
Before the party, take a side-view picture of your dog to a photo shop, and have it blown up into a big poster. (You can also draw a side view of your dog after taping several pieces of construction

paper together and then using markers to draw an outline of your dog's body and color it.) Use tape to hang the poster on a wall. Using colored construction paper that closely matches your dog's coloring, cut strips of paper that are one inch wide by four inches long. When it's time to play the game, write each guest's name on one of the tails, place tape on the end of each, and hand them out. The first player puts on a bandanna to cover her eyes. The other players turn her around a couple of times and then point her in the direction of the poster so she can place her tail on the birthday dog. After each guest has a turn, whoever places his or her tail closest to the dog's tail on the poster is declared the winner.

Although taping a tail to a picture may be awfully fun, remember never to tape or pin things on your favorite four-legged pal.

Run an Obstacle Course

Set up an obstacle course in your backyard.

Materials
* 3 chairs
* 1 timekeeper and judge
* 1 watch with a second hand
* 1 tennis ball
* 1 tennis racket
* 1 piece of paper
* Pen

Directions

Place the chairs in a row far enough apart so that you can run between them. Each player will run the obstacle course three times. The judge keeps track of the time of each player in each round of the game. For the first round, in turn, each player runs in a zigzag pattern around the chairs. For the

start

second round each player runs the same pattern but hops on one foot. For the third round each player runs in the same pattern but must bounce the tennis ball on the ground with the tennis racket while running. If a player loses control of the ball, he has to return to the spot where he lost control before he can continue bouncing the ball around the rest of the course. At the end of the game, the judge adds up the time of the three races, and the player who has the combined fastest time wins.

Option: You can play this game with the dogs if you make a couple of changes. First, each player should have his or her dog on a leash. Second, only run the obstacle course twice, and forget the tennis ball turn. Have each player make his or her dog sit before the judge stops the clock at the end of each round.

Play Musical Chairs with the Dogs

Here's a challenging variation on an old favorite.

Materials
* Chairs
* Dog leashes
* Judge
* Radio

Directions

Set up as many chairs as there are players to begin this game. Set up the chairs in a row with each facing the opposite direction of the previous one. Each player must have her dog on a leash. Appoint a judge to operate the radio. Begin the game by turning on the radio; each player begins to slowly walk her dog around the chairs. When the judge turns off the music, each player must find the closest chair and sit down and make her dog sit down, too. (Note: When you play this game with the dogs, you aren't officially sitting down until your dog is sitting down, too.) At the beginning of each round of this game, remove one chair so that after the first round you always have one chair fewer than the number of players. The judge operating the radio must break any ties for the same chair. The last sitting player and her dog win.

Important note: You'll be giggling a lot while you play this game, but remember not to scream. Screaming can overexcite the four-legged players.

Make a Dog-Food Cake

Another way to celebrate your dog's birthday is to make her a birthday cake. It's important to make a cake that your dog will like and that won't make her sick. People food is not made for a dog's digestive system, so chocolate cake is definitely out. Here's a recipe that you and your friends can try.

Ingredients
* 2 16-ounce cans of dog food
* ½ cup cooked white rice
* ½ cup dry dog food
* ¼ cup chopped carrots
* 1 box of dog bone biscuits

Utensils
* Can opener
* Bowl
* Spoon
* Springform cake pan
* Spatula

* Plate
* A lot of helping hands
* Serving spoon
* Paper plates

Directions
Open up the two cans of dog food and place the contents into the bowl. Add the cooked white rice and mix thoroughly. Spoon this mixture into the springform cake pan. Use the spatula to even out the food and make it smooth. Place the plate on the top of the cake pan, hold the two together, and quickly turn this upside down so that the plate is now on the bottom and the cake pan is upside down on the top. Tap around the sides of the cake pan to loosen the dog food. Unlatch the cake pan and carefully remove it from around the dog-food mixture. Remove the bottom of the pan, which is now resting on the top of the cake, by using the spatula to gently pull the bottom away from the dog-food mixture. Use helping hands to

apply the dry dog food and carrots on the sides and on the top of the cake. Place the cake in the refrigerator until it is time to serve.

When it's time to serve the cake, remove it from the refrigerator, let the birthday dog see it, and sing *Happy Birthday*. After the song, scoop portions of the cake onto paper plates. Give each dog guest a portion that fits his or her size. Place one dog bone biscuit on top of each piece of cake. All the dogs should be served at the same time, so you'll need to call out the helping hands again. You can serve the cake after playing the running games, and your happy party guests as well as the guest of honor will certainly take a nap after the cake is gone.

 ## Stop Green Tongue Before It Starts

Having a green thumb is a wonderful thing—helping plants grow, brightening your home, cleaning the air (because plants give off oxygen)—but a green tongue, when your dog eats your plants, is not. This is also unhealthy because many common household plants are poisonous to dogs. These include:

Amaryllis*	Castor bean	Ornamental yew	Rhubarb
Asparagus fern	Dieffenbachia	Philodendron	Umbrella plant
Azalea	Easter lily	Poinsettia*	Ivy, most types
Bird-of-paradise	Holly	Chrysanthemum	Mistletoe

*Neither of these plants will cause serious damage *if* you can get your dog to drink a lot of water after nibbling.

If you have these plants in your home, put them out of your dog's reach by hanging them from the ceiling or placing them on tall cabinets or dressers.

Stop the Begging

He looks so cute with his snout on the table and those sad eyes you haven't seen since he was a puppy. Don't do it! Don't give in. He'll learn that his behavior can get you to do what he wants—give him some of your food—so he'll do it again and see if it works again.

If you choose to give your dog table scraps, don't feed him directly from the table; otherwise you'll get to see those sad eyes every time you sit down to eat. If you must, give your dog finely cut up scraps after you're finished, preferably in his own bowl, mixed in with his own food, so that he'll be eating food that is nutritionally balanced for him, too.

Here are some solutions if you want to stop the begging behavior all together.

- Feed your dog just before you eat. If he's full, he's less likely to beg.

- Place a few coins in an aluminum can. Tape the opening shut. If he persists in hanging around the table, shake the can or drop the can on the floor. The noise should startle him enough to get him to leave the room. As soon as he stops doing the bad behavior, stop shaking or dropping the can. Be sure to praise him for stopping. This bad boy shaker can also work to help stop his barking when the postal carrier comes by.

- Place a squirt bottle on the table. If your dog comes too close, get him with a single squirt (don't douse him).

- Give a sharp "No!" without screaming, then put the dog in another room until mealtime is over. If necessary, shut the door to the room he's in. (Just remember to let him out after dessert.)

In the wintertime, you can give your dog a treat from summer if you plan ahead and create a nature box. Your dog will love fetching sticks or pinecones. You can remind her of summer by letting her smell the leaves or grass clippings you've saved.

Materials

* Shoe box or other small box with a lid
* Wrapping paper
* Crayons or markers
* Scissors
* Glue stick
* A bright sunny day
* Zip-top plastic freezer bags

Directions

Clean out any remaining paper or other objects from the shoe box. Lay some wrapping paper face down on a flat surface. Remove the lid of the shoebox and place it upside down on top of the paper. Trace around the outside of the box. Use scissors to cut this out and then glue it to the top of the shoebox. You can decorate your box even more by using crayons or markers to make designs on the sides or bottom. Use this box to store the nature items you collect.

On a bright sunny summer day, take your box outside to collect some natural treats for your pet. What you will find outside will vary depending on the region where you live, but here are some suggestions.

Sticks   Choose sticks that are thick enough so they won't break and long enough so your dog can carry one without being able to swallow it.

Leaves and grass   Collect a few leaves and a handful of grass and place them in a zip-top plastic freezer bag. Place these in the freezer until the middle of winter when you're ready to pull out your nature box for you and your dog to enjoy. Believe it or not, once you carefully thaw out these summer goodies, the grass will still be as fragrant and the leaves will be just as soft as when you placed them in the freezer.

Pinecones Pinecones are great for a few rounds of fetch before they start to fall apart. To play it safe, use a pinecone for a few rounds and then throw it away.

Dirt You can collect some dirt in a zip-top plastic freezer bag and let your dog exercise his sense of smell in the winter, too. What kind of face does your dog make when she smells the dirt?

When you've collected all your outdoor treats, bring the box back inside and share them with your dog either by leaving the items in the box or placing a bit of each on the floor (remember to pick up after yourself!) and having your dog nose through everything. When you're finished playing, you can store everything back in your box for your next nature hike without the walk!

  ## Hero Dog

Daisy was the golden retriever mascot for a Norwegian merchant ship that in 1944 was torpedoed during World War II in the North Atlantic. The torpedo sank the ship. Throughout the night Daisy swam among the survivors and went from man to man licking their faces to keep them awake in the icy ocean waters until they were rescued the next day.

  ## Stop Stomachaches

If you change the type of food you give your dog too quickly, he may get intestinal distress (an upset stomach). But over time this will pass without becoming a major problem. To help your dog avoid the bellyache, mix the new food with your dog's current food for a few days before making the final switch.

Bake Crunchy Dog Biscuits

These crunchy treats will help clean your dog's teeth.

Makes 24 biscuits

Ingredients

* 1 cup whole wheat flour
* 1 cup unbleached all-purpose flour plus extra for sprinkling on a countertop
* ½ cup cornmeal plus extra for rolling finished biscuits
* 2 tablespoons chopped parsley
* ½ teaspoon salt
* ¼ cup soy milk
* 1 cup chicken bouillon
* 4 tablespoons vegetable oil plus extra for coating the cookie sheet

Utensils

* 3 mixing bowls
* Large spoon for mixing
* Measuring cup
* Measuring spoons
* Small bowl
* Cookie sheet
* Fork
* Zip-top plastic freezer bag

Preheat the oven to 400°. In a bowl combine whole wheat flour, unbleached all-purpose flour, cornmeal, parsley, and salt. In a separate bowl, combine the soy milk, bouillon, and vegetable oil. In the empty bowl, pour one-third of the flour mixture and combine with one-third of the bouillon mixture; mix through. Pour another one-third of each mixture into this bowl and combine. Finally add the remaining amounts of each mixture in the combined bowl and mix thoroughly. Sprinkle some unbleached all-purpose flour on a clean countertop and knead the dough. Add additional flour on the countertop as necessary to prevent sticking.

Place about one-quarter cup cornmeal into the small bowl. Break off a Ping-Pong ball-size piece of dough and roll it into a ball. Place this ball into the cornmeal bowl and roll it around to coat the dough with cornmeal. Place all these balls on an oiled cookie sheet about one inch apart. Use the fork to press each ball down twice, making a criss-cross pattern on top.

Bake 20 minutes. Once all the treats are baked turn off the oven. Leave them in the oven for several hours to harden. Store biscuits in a zip-top plastic freezer bag in the refrigerator or, after one week, in the freezer. Let a treat from the freezer defrost for a few hours before giving it to your dog.

 ## An Important Four-Legged Member of the Lewis and Clark Expedition

Seaman, Meriwether Lewis's Newfoundland, rescued Lewis and several other members of the Lewis and Clark expedition team from a charging buffalo by pushing them out of its path and then driving the buffalo from the camp. Whew! Without Seaman, Lewis and Clark might not have been able to complete their charting of the Louisiana Purchase.

Make Yummy Dog Treats

All of the following treats use common household ingredients. Consequently, the treats don't have any preservatives, so they should be used within a day or placed in a zip-top plastic bag and frozen. If you freeze them and you want to treat your dog, let the treats sit out for a couple of hours to thaw before you give them to your pal.

Graham's Cookies

Here's a treat for your pooch that could've come right out of your grandma's kitchen.
Makes 30 cookies

Ingredients

* 2 cups graham cracker crumbs
* 1 cup unbleached all-purpose flour plus extra for sprinkling on a countertop
* 1 tablespoon baking powder
* ½ teaspoon salt
* ½ cup vegetable oil, plus extra for coating the cookie sheet
* ½ cup soy milk

Utensils

* Zip-top plastic freezer bag
* Wooden mixing spoon
* Measuring cup
* Measuring spoons
* Mixing bowl
* Thin, smooth drinking glass
* Baking sheet
* Plate

Directions

Preheat oven to 425°. Place 12 graham crackers in the zip-top bag and seal. Crush the graham crackers by using the palms of your hands or the back of a wooden mixing spoon. Measure out two cups of graham cracker crumbs and combine this with the flour, baking powder, and salt in the mixing bowl. Add the vegetable oil and mix through. Add the soy milk and mix through.

Lightly flour a kitchen countertop and pour out the dough. Knead the dough lightly, sprinkling more flour onto the countertop as needed to prevent dough from sticking. Use the glass to roll out

the dough until it's one-quarter-inch thick. Use the top of the glass to cut out cookies. Place the cookies one inch apart on a well-oiled baking sheet. Bake 12 minutes or until lightly browned and crispy.

Place cookies on a plate, cover, and keep them in the refrigerator. After one week, place any un-eaten treats in the freezer. You'll be able to give your dog a cookie from the freezer after you let it defrost for a few hours.

Sweet Raisin Dog Treats
You can make delicious treats for your pal in a jiffy. Better still, you might enjoy these, too. These tasty nibbles are courtesy of The Lion and the Lamb Pet Grooming Salon and More in Wilmington, Illinois.

Makes 12 to 14 treats

Ingredients
* 1 cup unbleached white flour
* ½ cup whole wheat flour
* ½ cup natural applesauce (without preservatives)
* ½ cup raisins
* Nonstick cooking spray

Utensils

* Mixing bowl
* Measuring cup
* Large spoon
* Cookie sheet
* 2 teaspoons
* Zip-top plastic freezer bag

In a small mixing bowl, blend the two flours together. Add the applesauce and mix until well blended. Add the raisins and mix through. (You can expect the batter to be a bit lumpy with all the raisins.)

Spray the cookie sheet with the nonstick spray. Drop the batter by teaspoonfuls onto the cookie sheet. When the tray is filled, turn the oven to 350°, and bake for 15 minutes. For soft, chewy treats, remove the tray from the oven after 15 minutes and let cool to room temperature before giving one to your dog. For slightly crunchy treats, turn off the oven after 15 minutes and let

the treats remain in the oven for 12 hours. For very crunchy treats, turn off the oven and let them sit in the oven for 24 hours.

Peanut Butter Yummies

You can make delicious peanut butter treats for your dog by following the Sweet Raisin Dog Treats recipe and substituting one-half cup natural peanut butter for the raisins. Remember to freeze the treats you don't give to your dog within a day in a zip-top plastic freezer bag.

Makes 12 to 14 treats

Pumpkin Treats for Special Dogs

Like people, dogs can be born with or develop allergies over time. Here's a recipe from The Lion and the Lamb Pet Grooming Salon and More that calls for spelt flour, which is available at health food stores. Spelt flour contains no gluten and no wheat—two common food sensitivities among animals.

Makes 12 to 14 treats

Ingredients

* 1½ cups plus a few pinches spelt flour
* ½ cup natural applesauce (without preservatives)
* ½ cup canned pumpkin (without preservatives)
* Nonstick cooking spray

Utensils

* Mixing bowl
* Measuring cup
* Large spoon
* Smooth drinking glass
* Cookie cutter
* Cookie sheet
* Zip-top plastic freezer bag

In a small mixing bowl, blend the flour and the applesauce. Add the pumpkin and mix until well blended.

Sprinkle some spelt flour on a clean countertop, on the glass, and on the cookie cutter. Place the dough on the dusted countertop, and use the glass to roll out the batter to one-quarter-inch thick. Use the dusted cookie cutter to cut out shapes, and place on a cookie sheet covered with nonstick cooking spray.

When the tray is filled, turn the oven to 350° and bake for 15 minutes. For soft, chewy treats,

 The Perfect Name

The basset hound got its name from the French word *bas*, meaning "low," and if you've ever seen this cuddly dog with droopy eyes and ears and its low-riding body, you'll know why the name fits this friendly breed.

remove the tray after 15 minutes and let cool to room temperature before giving one to your dog. For slightly crunchy treats, turn off the oven after 15 minutes and let the treats remain in the oven for 12 hours. For very crunchy treats, turn off the oven and let them sit in the oven for 24 hours.

These treats don't have any preservatives, so they should be used within a day or placed in a zip-top plastic freezer bag and frozen. Let a frozen treat defrost for a few hours before giving it to your pal.

Meaty Treats
Makes 16 to 18 treats

Ingredients
* 2 cups whole wheat flour
* ½ to 1 cup water
* ¼ pound ground beef

Utensils
* Mixing bowl
* Measuring cup
* Wooden spoon
* Smooth drinking glass
* Plastic knife
* Cookie sheet
* Metal spoon
* Zip-top plastic freezer bag

Preheat the oven to 350°. Place the flour in a bowl and add the water ¼ cup at a time, and mix through. Continue to add water until you have a thick but not watery flour and water paste. Add the ground beef and mix thoroughly. Place the mixture on a countertop and, using the drinking glass, roll the mixture out to about one-eighth inch thick. Use the glass top to make treats, or use the plastic knife to cut the flattened mixture into fun, funky shapes.

Place the treats on a cookie sheet and bake for 20 minutes. Check them after 10 minutes and then again after 15 minutes. You want the treats to be crunchy but not black or rock hard. To test for crunchiness, tap a treat with a metal spoon. If it sounds hard, take the treats out. Let them cool completely before serving a couple. Store the extras in a zip-top plastic bag in the freezer. Before giving your dog a treat from the freezer, let it defrost for a few hours.

Special Additions to Dog Food

Your dog's digestive system is different than yours. Adding some types of people food to your dog's food as a special treat is OK, but only if you do this once in a while. For example, you can add a little bit of warm gravy and mix it through your dog's food. (Remember to wash out his bowl after such a treat.) Here are some things you can add to and mix with your pal's food for a special occasion or once in a while just because.

- 1 scrambled egg
- ¼ cup grated cheese
- 1 tablespoon vegetable oil (This will also help keep his coat shiny and annoy pests like fleas.)
- Small amount of fruit such as bananas, pears, apples, grapes, and melons (popular with some dogs)
- Plain boiled rice
- Cooked pasta
- Carrots, finely chopped (also good for his breath)
- Cabbage, thinly sliced

Stop the Chewing

You have a ton of wonderful toys for your dog scattered around your home, so how come he chooses to chew on the corner of your couch or on your brand-new pair of tennis shoes? First, put your shoes away. Your dog can choke on the shoelaces, and unless he knows how to open up closet doors, they will be safe in your closet. Here are some other tips to help you stop the chewing.

- Rotate toys. Give your dog only a couple of toys at a time. Then change these every few days. It'll be like new toy treats all the time.

- Make some chicken or beef bouillon and soak some rubber toys in it. Once they've cooled and dried, watch your dog rediscover an old friend.

- Dab some peanut butter or cream cheese on an old familiar toy.

- Rub your hands all over a toy. Your dog loves you, and your scent is the next best thing to playing with you. This is a good thing to do before you leave for school in the morning, especially if your dog is a fairly new member of your family.

- When your dog starts to chew on the good stuff, be sure to praise him.

5

Play Time

Exercise is as good for you as it is for your dog. Just as your dog loves to walk, run, and jump, your body does, too, and exercising regularly will help keep you strong, healthy, and able to keep up with your four-legged friend.

Obedience Training

It's a good idea for you and your dog to take an obedience training class. Puppies as young as 12 weeks can attend special puppy classes. Obedience training is a good idea because it will give both you and your dog a chance to socialize and make new friends. Training will also help create a language between you and your dog so that you can understand each other and get along. Your dog wants to please you because when you are happy with him, you will praise him. Praise can be in the form of a gentle pat on the head maybe combined with the words "good dog," or it can be a dog biscuit or cookie. To behave well and earn this praise, your dog first needs to know what's expected of him. This is where obedience training helps.

When you find your dog chewing on the furniture, correct him. Don't yell or hit him. A firm "no" should be enough. If you hit your dog with your hand or a rolled-up newspaper, your dog will learn to stay away from you because being near you can cause pain. Hitting and yelling are punishments, not discipline. When your dog does something you want him to do, like not chewing the furniture, then praise him. This way you are shaping her behavior.

 Teach Her Young

You can establish your place as top dog by making your dog earn things she enjoys. Make her sit before you pet her. Make her give you her paw before feeding her. Obedience training at a young age will help your new pal learn the rules of your house and prevent behavior problems before they start.

To be effective, you can discipline your dog only when you catch her doing something wrong. If you come home from school and find a trash can knocked over and garbage all over the floor, all you can do is pick it up and hope you catch her in the act next time. If you forget and yell at her and shout "no" when you find the mess, she'll connect your "no" with the last thing that she was doing. Maybe she was just sleeping—no sleeping?—and maybe she knocked over the trash can four hours ago. She cannot connect your "no" now with something that she did so long ago.

Shaming is not an effective form of discipline either. For example, if your dog has an accident in the house, you cannot stick her nose in it and yell "no" and expect this behavior to change. Shame is connected to a conscience, and dogs don't have one. (See Chapter 1 for house-training tips.)

A Dog's Work Is Never Done

Dogs were originally domesticated in Eurasia between 12,000 and 14,000 years ago. Since then, dogs have earned their keep by helping their masters in a number of ways. They have been:

Watchdogs

Hunting companions

Flock guardians

Flock herders

Draft animals (to pull small carts or sleds)

Messengers in wartime

Injured-soldier locators

Seeing-eye dogs for people who are blind

Hearing dogs for people who are deaf

Assistants to people with disabilities

Illegal-drug sniffers

Rescue workers

Members of the family

Best friends

How does your dog earn her keep?

Teaching Discipline

Dogs learn best through repetition and consistency. When you are training your dog, use short words and be consistent—use the same word every time to mean the same thing, such as "heel" or "no." When your dog does not follow a command that you give him, such as "sit," you must correct him. A *correction* is not punishment but showing your dog how to respond correctly. If you are consistent, very quickly your dog will learn to work to avoid the correction and receive the praise.

Besides house training and teaching your dog good manners, there are only five commands that your dog really needs to know: sit, stay, heel, down, and come. You can teach your dog discipline with the help of an obedience training class or with the help of a book. However you choose to teach your dog, you should always be consistent, be patient, build on previous lessons, review often, and not give up.

Backyard Soccer

ake your dog into your fenced backyard for some fun and exercise with this activity.

Materials
* 4 large rocks, sticks, or some other large objects to mark the goalposts
* 1 large ball

Directions
Use rocks to mark each goalpost and the width of your soccer field. Drop the ball on the ground to begin play. Lightly kick the ball with the inside of your foot to move the ball forward. Use the bottom of the toe tip of your shoe to push the ball backward. When you get close enough to a goalpost, kick the ball through using your toe tip or the inside of your foot.

At first, your dog may just watch you run around the field chasing after a ball. Eventually your dog will begin to follow you around the yard, running and jumping to match your pace. She may even start to lead and get the ball away from you. If she manages to get the ball away from you, watch what she does.

 Play It Safe

Never kick the ball directly at your dog. This will not encourage her to play. Only when she sees you having fun and enjoying the activity will she then join you.

Toys for Safe Fun and Games

Here are the types of toys that are safe for your dog and that will definitely be enjoyed.

- Solid plastic bones
- Solid plastic animal toys
- Toys made out of thick, hard rubber, like a ball
- Big rawhide pieces
- A tennis ball

Toys to Avoid

- Latex toys that your dog can rip and swallow parts.

- Toys with squeaky noisemakers that can become loose and may be swallowed.

- Rawhide toys imported from other countries. The U.S. government (the Food and Drug Administration) regulates pesticide and preservative use in this country, but other countries don't always have such regulations.

- Animal bones of *any* kind. These can splinter and, if swallowed, can cause serious internal injury.

Be Top Dog and Stay Away from Tug-of-War Toys

The Anti-Cruelty Society doesn't recommend tug-of-war toys. Such toys are a way for your dog to challenge your authority. Your dog must always think that you're the leader to feel safe and protected. When you play tug-of-war with your dog, if you stop and walk away because you're tired or bored, your dog will think this means he wins. The more you play tug-of-war games and walk away when you get bored, the more this feeling will be reinforced in your dog. Eventually, your dog will consider himself the leader, and your attempts to discipline him may be ignored. Tug-of-war toys also can encourage biting behavior. Tug-of-war toys are *only* OK *if* they are used between dogs. Let them challenge each other's place in the pack. With you out of the competition, you'll always remain top dog!

Teach Your Dog to Sing

ogs sometimes learn by imitation. If there's something that you often do, like sing, your dog may want to join in the fun.

When your dog barks or starts to howl, go into the same room with him and try to imitate the sound he's making with your own voice. At first, this may make your dog stop making these sounds, especially if he usually gets in trouble for barking too much. Imitate your dog's sounds as often as you can for a week. In the second week, again imitate the howling and barking sounds your dog makes and try to bend or extend those sounds into words. For example, when your dogs makes the sound "owww," you can make this sound too and then add on with "owww dry I am." "Ruff" can become "ruff rover red rover send (your dog's name) right over." In the third week, whenever your dog makes a barking or howling sound, whatever song these sounds remind you of, begin to sing it. Add in a few howls like your dog makes in the middle of the lyrics. When she starts to join in the fun, be sure to praise her so that she'll know she's doing what you want.

Taking regular walks is good exercise and gives you both a chance to stretch out and enjoy the outdoors. Whether you have a dog or a puppy, be sure to take him for walks in all kinds of weather—sun, wind, rain, and snow—so he can experience it all. Remember the first time you took a walk in the rain? Let your dog have this same magical experience. Just be sure to dry yourself and your dog completely when you go indoors.

If you need to walk your dog so that he can go to the bathroom, try to take him out at the same time every day, such as first thing in the morning, just after you get home from school, and after dinner. It's important to keep a regular schedule.

 Play It Safe

Dog owners who live in high-rise buildings should not use a retractable leash in the elevator. Carry a regular nylon leash for the elevator ride home to be safe.

It's important to always put your dog on a leash when you take her outside (this is not necessary in a fenced yard). Here are five good reasons why.

1. For your dog's own safety, to make sure he doesn't go into the street unless you have looked both ways.

2. To be respectful of other people's property, so your dog can't go sniff around someone else's flower bed unless the homeowner says it's OK.

3. Helps prevent fights with other dogs.

4. Helps you control the area where your dog roams to prevent him from getting burrs or worse.

5. Prevents your dog from running away.

 A Good Walking Tool

A retractable dog leash is a good alternative to the traditional leash because it gives you more control. You can get a retractable dog leash that extends from 6 feet (for use in cities) to extra-long ones extending up to 26 feet; however, the average length is about 16 feet. With a push of the button, you can shorten the leash, even if your dog isn't interested in slowing down. This can come in handy when a car, another dog, or young children are approaching.

Frisbee and Flyball Fun

Here are two team sports that you and your dog can play together.

Frisbee

The ALPO Canine Frisbee Disc Championships are held in communities throughout the United States. Everyone is welcome to compete, and there is no entry fee. Discs are provided. For a free copy of the guidelines, training manual, throwing tips, plus a calendar of events, contact:

ALPO Canine Frisbee Disc Championship
4060-D Peachtree Road, #326G
Atlanta, GA 30319
(800) 786-9240

Flyball

Flyball is a competitive relay race involving hurdle-jumping and ball-retrieving. It's becoming wildly popular. Originally created in 1975, there are more than 7,000 dogs currently compete in flyball competitions with their handlers.

Flyball is a sport where two teams of four dogs race against each other while completing an obstacle course. The flyball course is 51 feet long. One dog at a time runs over four hurdles to a box. The dog then hits the box and grabs the tennis ball and returns back over the hurdles to the handler. As soon as the first dog is finished, the next dog goes. Whichever team has the best finishing time, after completing the course properly, wins.

The North American Flyball Association (NAFA) has a registry of the more than 290 clubs across the United States. You can write to the address below or call to find clubs in your area. Many of these clubs have both child and adult members.

NAFA
1400 W. Devon Avenue
Box 512
Chicago, IL 60660
(309) 688-9840

 Agility Games Are Good Fun

Agility games such as Frisbee, flyball, fetch, and running an obstacle course are not only good exercise for your dog but will also teach her good flexibility, keep her fit, and improve her ability to follow instructions. (See Chapter 4 for an obstacle course game.)

Fetch

ames like fetch encourage your dog to use her brain, not just her muscles.

Materials

✱ 1 tennis ball

Directions

Let your dog smell the tennis ball, and, when you're certain that you have her attention and she is following the ball with her eyes, throw it a few feet away from you. Encourage your dog to go get it and bring it to you with only a few words. Crouch down to the ground to encourage your dog to look at you. When she looks at you, look at the ball you've thrown, point to it, and say, "go get it" followed by your dog's name. Repeat this three times. If your dog is still not attempting to fetch the ball, walk over to the ball and try it again in another direction. Again, repeat the sequence to encourage her to bring you the ball. If after three times she is still

not responding, throw the ball in her direction, and then encourage her to come to you with the ball. You can also show her what you want. You can throw the ball, run to it, pick it up, and bring it to your dog by dropping it on the ground in front of her. You may need to try this every day for a week to get her interest and understanding.

Remember to praise her for any interest she shows in this fetching activity, such as looking in the direction of the ball, sniffing the ball, or picking up the ball.

Bring It, Throw It, Go Get It, Drop It

Teaching your dog to drop something from her mouth when you say so is good because she may pick up something you don't want her to have, like one of your toys. If you teach your dog to drop something, you won't have to get near her mouth with your hands. This is safer for you, too.

Hide and Go Seek

Playing hide and go seek is a fun way to teach your dog to solve problems.

Materials
* You
* Your dog

Directions
Start out simply by running into a room and hiding behind a door. If your dog doesn't run after you, call her name or whistle softly. After a few times, you can make the finding more difficult by hiding in a closet or under a bed.

When your dog finds you, praise her by giving her a pat on the head and saying "good girl" (or "good boy"). Let her hear the joy in your voice and know that she has pleased you. If she enjoys the reward (the praise), she'll want to please you again to get more.

Playtime Is Fun Time

If you have a slide in your backyard, some dogs may give sliding a try.

Jumping through a hula hoop is another fun follow-the-leader trick.

Never force your dog to do anything he doesn't want to do. Playtime is fun time!

Bury Bones Together

You can teach your dog to bury bones in your yard as long as it's not near any flower beds or other landscaping.

Materials
* 1 garden shovel
* Some dog biscuits

Directions
Go into your backyard with your dog and find a soft part of the lawn. Use the shovel to dig a hole three inches deep. Once you've dug the hole, let your dog smell the bone and watch you place it in the hole. Then cover it lightly with the dirt. Step back and see what your dog does. Does she sniff around the hole? Does she walk away without interest? Does she start to dig in the same spot to get the bone? If your dog doesn't react, take another biscuit and crumble it up on top of the covered bone. Lead your dog to this spot and see if she's more interested. If you still aren't getting any reaction from your dog, dig up the bone so half of it is uncovered. Lead your dog back to the spot and see what she does. If she still could not care less, just leave it. Maybe tomorrow she'll be more interested in the biscuit.

Scenting Games

Dogs have a powerful sense of smell. A dog's sense of smell helps him understand objects that he encounters in the world, like you, other dogs, dog food, grass, and more.

Materials
✱ You
✱ Your dog
✱ Treats
✱ Dog food crumbs

Directions
Hide treats around your house and see how many your dog can find. You may have to make a trail of dog food crumbs leading to where you've hidden the dog bones or other treats. Or, you can put the bone or rawhide treat under his nose so he can smell it, then let him follow you with his eyes to see where you place it, such as under a rug or behind a door. Then leave that area and see if your dog goes for it.

Learn the Language of Dogs

Just like humans, dogs let you know how they feel, what they think, or what they want by their body language.

When your dog comes up to you and puts his head in your lap and looks up at you with a sweet face, don't be fooled. He isn't sad; he's trying to get you to pet him. Go ahead if you feel like it. But know that if your dog does this many times and you respond by petting him, he'll learn that he's the leader and he can get you to do what he wants by giving you this sweet look and his head in your lap. A firm "no" and not petting him will, over time, teach him to stop doing this.

If you are taking an obedience class with your dog and she sits on your feet and turns her head away from you, this means that she's not interested in what you're trying to teach her. This is not a good body position for learning.

Subtle changes in the position of their ears, tail, mouth, face, hair, and posture will give you the clues you need to understand the message your dog is sending you. Some examples are: a calm dog will have relaxed ears and tail; a dominant dog will stare directly at you in your eyes; and a submissive dog will avoid direct eye contact with you.

Here's some more dog body language and the meaning of each posture:

Active Submission
When a dog lies on her back, this means she knows you're the leader and she's friendly and wants you to slowly approach her.

Passive Submission
A dog on all fours with a wagging tail knows you're the leader and will come to you if you call her nicely.

Play Bow

When your dog looks like he's bowing to you with front paws extended out and his behind up in the air with his tail wagging, this is an invitation to play.

Fear

When he is bending down slightly with ears pressed back against his head, showing his teeth, growling, and tucking his tail between his legs, this means he's defensive and will be unpredictable. Stay away!

Dogs make five types of sounds that mean different things.

When a dog is:	He'll make a sound like this:
Lonely or sad	Infant cry, whimper, or whine
Warning you	Growl or sharp bark
Trying to get attention	Plaintive bark or howl
In pain	Yip, yelp, or scream
Experiencing pleasure	Moan

Aggression

A dog sticking her tail straight up, putting her ears up and forward, showing her teeth, and growling doesn't recognize you as the leader, and she may attack you. Stay away!

Cut the Racket!

If your dog starts to bark too much, instead of getting mad, get her to stop. Here are some tips to keep the peace.

- Exercise your dog more often. A lot of exercise will eventually get you a tired dog; that is, if your energy can outlast hers.

- Say a firm "quiet," but don't yell.

- Get her some new chew toys.

- Rub your hands over a new toy and present it to your dog. If she's barking because she misses you, your scent will help keep her company.

- Leave the room. If there's no audience, maybe the barking performance will stop.

- Praise your dog more often. If she's barking to get your attention, giving it to her more often might be the off switch you're searching for.

- OK, here's that old favorite again, the one that dogs hate and should be used sparingly—place a few coins in an empty aluminum can and tape the opening shut. In an emergency or if you've tried other techniques and nothing seems to work, shake the can or drop it on the floor about three feet from your dog. (Don't do it too close to her, or you may hurt her ears.)

Dog-Day Story

This is a fun way to exercise your creative spirit as well as your body and give your dog some good exercise time, too. This is a great rainy-day way to take your dog for a walk and still keep dry.

Materials
* Paper
* Pencil
* Your imagination
* Room to run around

Directions
Make a list of three places that you would like to visit with your dog, such as a field of wildflowers, your grandmother's house, and a lumberyard. Next, make a list of three sounds, such as a bird's chirp, the ring of a telephone, and laughter. Finally, make a list of three actions or situations, such as drinking tea at a tea party, tying your shoes, and planting a garden.

Now you have all the tools to write your dog-day story. The object is to use your list of places, sounds, and actions in your story and to make it as active as possible so when you act out the story, your dog will have fun, too!

Take a minute to imagine that you are visiting these three places, hearing these three sounds, and being in these three situations with your dog at your side. What might happen? What kinds of things will you and your dog need to do in each place? How will your story end? Once you've written your story, act it out!

Here's an example to get your started. This story uses all the examples listed above. See how wild and crazy your story gets!

119

Yesterday, I was sleeping when the phone rang (brring, brring). My dog Molly and I jumped out of bed to answer it (lie down and then jump up and pretend to pick up a phone). It was Grandma. She was calling to invite us over to feed the birds and have tea in her garden. I hung up the phone, got dressed, put on Molly's leash, and we were out the door (hang up the phone, pretend to put on clothes including socks and shoes with laces that need to be tied, attach your dog's leash, and go out a pretend door).

Molly and I walked through a field of wildflowers to get to Grandma's house (walk around). We stopped along the way to smell the flowers, and Molly even rolled around in them (pretend to smell the pretty flowers). She looked so happy; I laughed and started rolling around in the flowers with her (laugh and roll around on the floor, and, who knows, maybe your dog will, too).

We finally got to the edge of the field and then passed a lumberyard. Molly and I saw a big man with a handlebar mustache in the lumberyard (show your handlebar mustache while you pretend to chop some wood). We waved to him, he waved back, and then we continued on to Grandma's house (smile, wave, and walk on).

We walked some more, and then we ran for a while, and before we knew it we were at Grandma's door, and so we knocked (walk around, then run, and then knock on a door or pretend to). Grandma answered the door and hugged me and patted Molly on the head. We walked into her kitchen, and she asked me to carry the sugar and milk out to the garden. She carried the tea tray that had a bowl of water on it for Molly (pretend to walk into a kitchen and carry sugar and milk outside—don't forget to open the screen door). Molly and Grandma came outside, and we sat in her garden (help your dog through the door and sit). Grandma asked me to serve the tea, so I poured some into each cup, added sugar and milk just like we like it, and gave Grandma her cup of tea (pour tea, add sugar and milk, stir the tea, and serve it). I placed the bowl of water on the ground for Molly, and then I sat down to enjoy my cup of tea (place a pretend bowl of water on the floor and sit down, pick up your cup of tea, and drink).

Grandma asked me how school was, and as I talked the birds began chirping (chirp like a bird). Grandma said they were telling us how their day was, too.

After we finished our tea, Grandma asked me to help her plant some flowers in her garden. Molly and I spent the rest of the day digging holes in Grandma's yard (dig a few holes with your pretend shovel, and place a flower in the hole, cover it up with dirt, and water it; pretend to dig a hole the way your dog does). My holes were along the flowerbed, but Molly's holes were everywhere. Grandma planted flowers in Molly's holes, too. When we were finished Grandma thanked us and kissed us both.

The end.

Circus Fun

You and your dog can clown around with this game. How high you build these will depend on your dog's size and agility (how easily he moves or how high he jumps). Use sturdy boxes and crates for this activity. When you're ready, put on a show for your family and friends.

Materials
* Plastic or metal milk crates
* Sturdy boxes
* Chairs

Directions
Start out with a single milk crate. Show your dog what you want him to do by doing the action first. With the single milk crate, start by walking around it. Next, do it again but call your dog's name, and see if he'll follow you. Do it again by calling his name, waiting until he comes to you, then encouraging him to walk around the crate with you. If he does what you want him to, be sure to reward him with a pat on the head. Then give him a treat and tell him he was good.

Once he's mastered this, add on another step—walk around the crate and then jump up on top of it. Follow the same three steps to get him to do this: show him what you want, call his name, and do it again for him to see. Then call his name again and wait for him to come and have him follow you in the action.

You can keep adding actions to this single crate, or you can add another box of a different size, showing him how to circle them both and then jumping on top of one box and then the other box. Be sure to reward him whenever he does what you want. You don't have to give him a food treat every time, but just as you like to hear

123

encouraging words such as "Good job!" and "Well done!", your dog likes to hear those words, too.

Don't be discouraged if he doesn't follow you the first time. Practice and patience will win him over.

Option: Place two chairs on the floor with the backs up in the air and with the tips of the backs facing and touching so that they form a little tunnel. Crawl through the space first to show your dog how to do it, then try to get him to follow you through the tunnel.

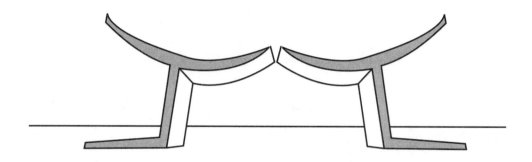

Chairs should touch to form a tunnel.

124

6

Show & Tell Treats

This chapter is filled with special treats that you can make for yourself. You can be with your dog all day long—even when you have to go to school—when you make a medal-lion, or you can take your scrapbook to school for show and tell or to share with your friends on the playground.

Make a Scrapbook

This is a great show-and-tell item. You can record your life with your dog using pictures and stories. (See Keep a Pet Journal activity in this chapter.) Then, as you look back through the book, figure out who has changed more, you or your dog.

Materials
* Newspapers
* 1 yard fabric
* 1 spiral notebook with a hard (not plastic) cover
* Ruler
* Marker
* Scissors
* Craft glue that works on fabric, too
* 100-percent polyester fiberfill
* Lace trim (optional)

Directions

Spread out newspapers on a tabletop. Lay the fabric on the table with the pattern facing down. Open the notebook with the spiral center face up. Use the ruler and marker to measure a four-inch fabric border on every side of the notebook. Draw this box on the fabric using the marker, and cut out the fabric box. This piece of fabric will be the cover of your notebook.

Next, cut out two pieces of fabric for the inside of your notebook. Using your closed notebook as a guide, trace around the outside of your notebook. Use the ruler to measure a box that's one inch smaller all around the vertical and horizontal edges of your notebook. This piece of fabric should be smaller than one side of your notebook. Cut one more piece of fabric exactly the same size for the other inner side of your notebook. These two pieces of fabric, the endsheets, will cover the inside of the notebook.

On the left side of the notebook, glue one vertical side of the fabric to the notebook.

Next, cut the fabric at the spine (where the spiral metal clips are) so that you can glue the top and bottom parts of the fabric on the left side of the notebook to the interior just as you did with the vertical-side fabric. Remember to leave the cloth loose enough so that you have space for the notebook to bend on the spine and close. Pull the fabric on the bottom horizontal edge up toward the center of the notebook. With your other hand, feel

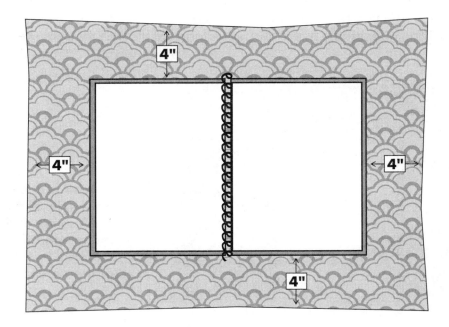

for the closest edge of the metal spine and use the marker to draw a line from the top edge of the fabric to the edge of the notebook along the line of this spine. Cut the fabric along this line. Glue this horizontal flap of fabric on top of the other flap of fabric you previously glued. Repeat these steps for the top edge of the notebook. Next, center one of the endsheets on the inside cover of the notebook. Glue it in place, making sure that you glue down all the edges. The left side of the notebook should now be covered with fabric on both the inside and the outside.

Wait for the glue to dry (usually one hour). Stuff the space between the side of the notebook with the glued fabric and the notebook with the fiberfill. Start filling the bottommost part first, pushing the fiberfill down into the corners. Fill it all the way to the spine.

Bend the notebook closed to judge how much fabric you must leave to cover the spine and still allow the notebook to close easily. Mark this place on the fabric with your marker and cut the fabric from the outermost edge of the fabric to the

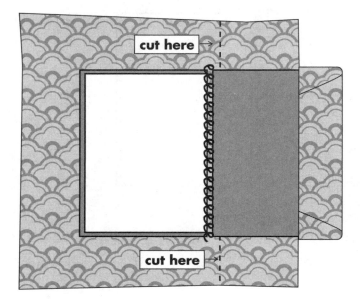

Cut the fabric on the right side of the notebook spine and glue the created flap of material to the interior of the notebook.

spine. Repeat this for the other edge of the notebook. Pull these little flaps of fabric inside the notebook and glue each to one side of the spine.

Glue the top and bottom edges of the fabric to the right side of the notebook and allow the glue to dry. Stuff the interior between the fabric and the notebook with fiberfill. Glue the vertical flap down and allow it to dry. Finally, center the last

endsheet on the inside cover of the notebook. Glue it in place, making sure that you glue down all the edges. The right side of the notebook should now be covered with fabric on both the inside and the outside.

You can decorate your scrapbook by gluing a lace trim to the outer border all along the notebook.

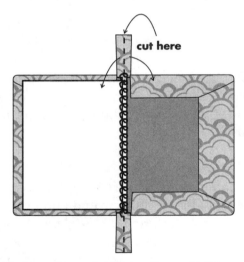

Cut fabric strip as indicated, and glue to both sides of the interior spine.

Cut a piece of fabric that is one inch smaller than the dimensions of the notebook. This will be the endsheet. Glue to the inside front cover, concealing the glued flaps. Repeat for the inside back cover after stuffing the cover with fiberfill.

Whether you get a dog when she's a puppy or when she's an adult, the way your dog looks, behaves, eats, sleeps, and smells—everything—will change over time. By keeping a pet journal you can keep track of the funny and significant events in your dog's life.

Materials
* Notebook paper
* Section dividers
* 1 3-ring notebook (This makes it easy to add or eliminate pages.)
* Favorite pen, marker, or pencil
* Scotch tape
* Markers, ribbons, glitter, or stickers

Directions
Place all the sheets of notebook paper in the notebook. Use the section dividers to categorize the events in your dog's life. Use the following categories:

Doggie Data
Write your dog's name and address here. How did he get to your house? Did you adopt him? Did you buy him from a breeder? What was the date? What kinds of cool things could your dog do when you first got him? Did he know any tricks? Was he a house-trained puppy? You can keep a record of how much he eats and what he eats here, too. You can also list any food allergies your dog has and tell how you learned about these sensitivities. Did he come with allergies? Or did he develop them later in his life?

Fun and Games
Here you can include new tricks and games learned. List each trick he learned and every game you played, and include the dates if you can remember them. Did anything funny happen when you were trying to teach him the new trick? Was anyone else playing the game with you?

Obedience Training

Tell how you taught your dog each command and how long it took him to learn it. Include the dates of your lessons and when he mastered each command. To keep your dog obedience trained, you need to periodically review what he's learned. You can keep track of these dates using your journal. You can also record how you praised your dog after learning each command so that you can continue to praise him in the same way.

Naughty Dog

What lessons did your dog learn the hard way? What happened, and who discovered the dog doing this naughty thing (for example, drinking out of the toilet bowl or digging up a flowerbed)?

Silly Stuff

What funny things has your dog done? When does he make you laugh? When does he make other people laugh?

Keepsake Days

This is a good place to record those special, very fun days that you share with your dog, like going on a wilderness hike or entering a flyball competition.

Health and Fitness

Here's where you can list the amazing feats your dog has done, like leaping over a tall building in a single bound or completing a record number of push-ups (and be sure to call the *Guinness Book of World Records* while you're at it). Did your veterinarian recommend that your dog lose or gain weight? All of these tidbits go here.

Guest Book

This section is for other family members or friends who would like to share a funny story or a trick they taught your dog. They can also write sweet messages to your dog that you can read to him.

Decorate each section divider by taping a photo of your dog doing something typical for that category (for example, catching a Frisbee under "Fun and Games"), or you can draw your dog performing some miraculous feat that you want to teach him, or you can decorate it in your own unique way by using markers, ribbons, glitter, or stickers.

Doggone Stars

Dogs are actors, too! Have you ever heard of a four-legged star named Eddie? He's the Jack Russell terrier who shares the spotlight with the other stars on *Frasier*. Prior to making it in Hollywood, Eddie had been given away a couple of times by different owners. Here are some other famous canines that you may have heard of or seen.

- **Rin Tin Tin**—This German shepherd had a silent movie career for 14 years and then starred in 22 black-and-white films.

- **Lassie**—Lassie starred in his own television show for 17 years.

- **Benji**—His movies have grossed more than $100 million. Benji and his son Benji II were inducted into the American Humane Society's Animal Actors' Hall of Fame.

- **Mike**—This blue- and brown-eyed dog appeared in *Down and Out in Beverly Hills*. Mike has a star and a paw print on the Hollywood Walk of Fame.

 Movies That Have Gone to the Dogs

Here are some doggone great movies.

Beethoven	*Lady and the Tramp*
Benji	*Lassie Come Home*
Benji the Hunted	*Old Yeller*
Digby—The Biggest Dog in the World	*101 Dalmatians*
	The Shaggy Dog
Doctor Dolittle	*Turner & Hooch*
K-9	

133

Who's in the Doghouse?

You can put anyone in your family in the doghouse with this activity.

Materials
* 1 piece of thin cardboard
* Pencil
* Scissors
* 1 4-by-6-inch or larger sheet of magnetic paper (available at office supply stores)
* Construction paper
* Markers
* Yarn
* Craft glue

Directions
Draw a doghouse with a big doorway on the piece of cardboard. Cut this out. Place the cardboard doghouse on top of the magnetic paper. Use the pencil to trace around the cardboard doghouse. Cut out the magnetic paper. Place your cardboard doghouse on top of the construction paper, trace it, and cut this out. This will be the front of your doghouse. Use markers and yarn to decorate the front of the doghouse; maybe even write "doghouse" over the doorway. Glue the decorated construction paper doghouse to the cut-out magnetic doghouse. Allow this to dry. Select a photograph of your dog, you, a friend, or family member, and use the magnetic doghouse to frame it. You can hang your doghouse on the refrigerator, washing machine, dryer, or metal cabinet.

Wear Your Dog Close to Your Heart

You and your dog can go everywhere together if you make a medallion and put his picture on it.

Materials
* Coffee cup or glass
* 1 piece of cardboard
* Pencil
* Scissors
* 1 photograph of your dog (or a picture of you and your dog)
* Newspaper
* Acrylic paint
* Paintbrush
* Craft glue
* Toothpick
* Glitter
* Yarn or ribbon

Directions

Place the coffee cup or glass on top of the piece of cardboard, trace around it, and cut it out. Choose a favorite photograph of your dog or you and your dog, and cut a circle around the image. (Option: You can cut out the image around the outline of you and your dog.)

Spread out some newspaper on a table and paint the cardboard circle. Wait for this to dry, and then glue the back of the photograph and place this on the painted cardboard circle. Squirt some glue on the newspaper, and dip the toothpick in it; use this like a pencil to write your name and your dog's name with the glue on the cardboard. Sprinkle glitter on top of the glue, wait a few seconds, and then lift up the medallion and shake off all the extra glitter. (Note: If you are using fast-drying glue, write one glue letter at a time and then apply the glitter.)

Once the medallion is completely dry, use the pencil or scissors to poke a hole in the top and string the yarn through it. Hang it around your neck and decide how low you'd like your medallion to hang. Cut the yarn about two inches longer. Tie it in a knot, and the medallion's ready to wear.

  ## Popular Pooches

According to the 1996 American Kennel Club records, the six most popular breeds are:

1st: Labrador retriever
2nd: Rottweiler
3rd: German shepherd
4th: Golden retriever
5th: Beagle
6th: Poodle

  ## Ready, Place, Dog Show!

Did you know that the second oldest sporting event in the United States is the Westminster Kennel Club Dog Show? Second only to the Kentucky Derby in age, this competition features 2,500 dogs and occurs every February at Madison Square Garden in New York City.

Make a Dog Mobile

You can hang this mobile above your bed or desk. If you hang it above your bed, it'll be the first thing you see when you wake up and will help remind you to feed your dog and make sure she has plenty of fresh, clean drinking water.

Your dog mobile can include pictures of many of the things that are important to keep your dog happy and healthy.

Materials
* Paper
* Pen or pencil
* Crayons, markers, or colored pencils
* Scissors
* Cardboard, several pieces
* Craft glue
* 1 hanger
* Construction paper
* Paper clips, 1 for each object
* Clay, less than a fistful

* Spool of thread
* Scotch tape
* 1 thumbtack

Directions
On the paper, draw pictures of many of the things that are important to your dog. Here are some ideas: a collar, a leash, a food bowl, a water bowl, the sun, the grass, a grooming brush, you, and a veterinarian.

After you're finished drawing all the objects, color them, then cut each object out. Place each object on top of a piece of cardboard, trace around it, and cut out the cardboard. Glue the paper picture to the cardboard. Place the hanger on top of a piece of construction paper, and trace around the interior of the triangle. Cut this out. Do this a second time. Write your dog's name on one triangle and your name on the other.

Bend the outside arm of each paper clip. Use this sharp point to poke a hole through the top of each picture and pull the paper clip through the hole. Bend the paper clip arm back up, and break off a little piece of clay to cover the sharp tip of each paper clip. Next, unwind the thread and thread it through the remaining loop of the paper clip. Tie this end in a knot around the paper clip. Cut the string to your desired length and tie the other end to the horizontal arm of the hanger. Cut the strings to various lengths so that some objects will hang lower than others. To keep your objects evenly spaced, place little bits of clay on either side of the string when every piece is hanging where you want it. Tape the construction paper triangles to each side of the hanger.

Once all the cardboard pictures are hung on the hanger, tie a string to the neck of the hanger and wrap the other end around a thumbtack. Push the thumbtack into your ceiling. Lie down and enjoy your artwork.

 Dog Duties

Dogs have helped people get their work done for hundreds of years. Here are some new ways that dogs are earning their keep.

Dogs are companions for older citizens. People who are older sometimes get lonely and need to feel safe, even in their own homes. A dog can help provide this comfort and security.

Border collies are being used by some golf courses to help keep geese away. Because they herd with their eyes instead of barking, this is good for the golfers, who are concentrating on sinking putts.

Border collies are also being used to keep geese out of corporate parks and away from office buildings.

Write to a Dog Pen Pal

Did you recently move? Or did a friend and her dog move away not too long ago? If your dog has a playmate that she hasn't seen in a while, you can help her keep in touch with her buddy.

Materials
* Paper
* Pen or marker
* 1 or more recent photographs of you and your dog
* Dog stickers
* Dog biscuits
* 1 padded envelope
* Postage stamps
* Playmate's address

Directions
Write a letter to your friend and ask her to read it to her dog. In the letter include details of your life, such as funny things that have happened lately to you and your dog, tricks your dog has learned, and new parks you've visited. Read the letter to your dog. You can include her reactions in a postscript (PS). Send along a picture of you and your dog, and ask your pal to send one in return. Place the letter, some dog stickers (for your friend), and some dog biscuits (for your dog's friend) into a padded envelope. Address the outside of the envelope, and attach the correct amount of postage (ask an adult for help with this). If there's a post office box nearby, put the leash on your dog, walk to the post office box, and mail the letter together.

 Paws for Thought

According to the American Pet Products Manufacturers Association, in 1996 U.S. consumers spent $21 million on dog products.

❖ Frame Your Four-Legged Friend ❖

Here's a way to see your dog the very first thing in the morning and the very last thing at night if you place this picture frame on your nightstand or dresser by your bed.

Materials

❋ Ruler
❋ 1 8½-by-11-inch piece of cardboard
❋ Pencil
❋ Scissors
❋ 1 picture of you and your dog
❋ 1 sheet of unlined white paper, such as typing or computer paper
❋ Newspaper
❋ Acrylic paint
❋ Paintbrush
❋ Tiny trinkets, such as plastic stars, favorite beads, or rhinestones
❋ Buttons (some craft shops have dog buttons)
❋ Yarn
❋ Craft glue

Directions

Use the ruler to measure five and one-half inches from the short edge of the cardboard, near the middle, and mark this place with a pencil dot. Measure this two more times above and below your original dot so you have three pencil dots on the cardboard. Draw a line to connect these dots. Cut the cardboard on this line. This will give you two equal-size pieces of cardboard. Place the photograph in the center of one of the pieces of cardboard. Trace around the photograph. To make sure the photograph can be seen through but not fall out of the picture frame window, measure one-fourth inch all the way around the photograph outline you just traced. Draw a box that measures one-fourth inch smaller than the photograph. Once this smaller box is traced, erase the original photograph box lines. Use the sharp point of the scissors to poke a hole through the cardboard inside the remaining box. Completely cut out this box.

Place your picture frame on the sheet of plain white paper. Trace the outline and interior box of your frame onto the paper. Set this aside.

Spread out sheets of newspaper on top of a table, and place your cardboard picture frame on top. Use your favorite color acrylic paint to paint a pretty background color for your

picture frame. Let the paint dry completely.

While your frame is drying, use the traced picture frame on the white sheet of paper to plan how you will decorate your frame. Arrange all the trinkets, buttons, and yarn that you would like to use. When your painted picture frame is dry, use the craft glue to place your gems as you did on the white paper.

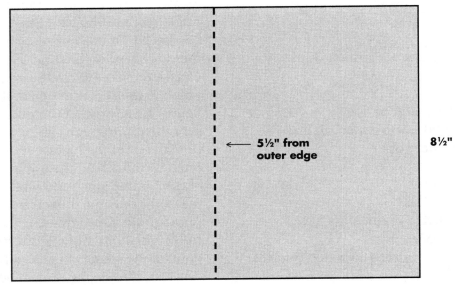

←— **5½" from outer edge**

8½"

11"

Once everything is completely dry, glue three sides of the back of the picture frame and stick it to the other side of your original piece of cardboard. Leave one side unglued so that you can slip the picture into the frame. After a while, as you and your dog grow, you can change the picture in your frame.

Option: Squirt some craft glue onto a corner of the newspaper and dip a toothpick into the glue.

Use this toothpick to write the name of your dog on your picture frame. Sprinkle glitter over the glue letters to completely cover them. Wait a few minutes and then lift and tap the frame over the newspaper. All the unglued glitter should fall, and what will remain is your dog's name in glitter on the frame. (Note: If you're using fast-drying glue, write only one or two letters at a time and then apply the glitter before continuing.)

KIRBY

1/4"

frame

photograph outline

cut here

Measure and cut out ¼ inch less on all sides of the photograph tracing

143

Paint Your Dog's Portrait

For Queen Victoria's 17th birthday in 1836, her mother, the Duchess of Kent, had a portrait of her spaniel, Dash, painted by Sir Edwin Henry Landseer. Overnight everyone wanted to have a portrait of his or her pet. You can paint a portrait of your dog, too.

Materials
❋ Instant camera or photo of your dog
❋ Paper
❋ Pencil
❋ Crayons, markers, watercolors, or
   tempera paint
❋ Scissors

Directions
If you have an instant camera, take a picture of your dog when he is sleeping, resting, or playing. If you don't have this type of camera, look for a picture of your dog in your family photo album. Study the picture and take note of the colors in the scene, the setting (location where the photo was taken), and what your dog is doing. Now you're ready to start sketching the picture onto a sheet of paper using the pencil. Are you in the picture? Would you like to be? Then go ahead, draw yourself in—you're the artist!

Once you have your dog portrait and any other images re-created on the paper, color or paint it. You can use natural, realistic colors or wild, bizarre colors to dress up your portrait.

Option: You can make your art 3-D. If your dog has a ball in his mouth, draw the same size ball on a piece of construction paper, or color a piece of paper and cut it out. Cut a strip of paper that is narrower than the object and one inch long. For example, if the ball is one-half inch across, cut a strip that is one-quarter-inch wide and one inch long. Fold the strip like a tiny accordion. Glue

one end to the back of the ball (object) and the other to the picture on top of the original object you painted. Repeat this process for as many items in the portrait as you want.

 The Object of Art

The poodle has appeared in more works of art than any other breed of dog.

Can-Do Canine Show

Think back to the first time you played with your dog. Did he jump all over you and lick your face? Did he come when you called his name? Did he know his name? Could he do any tricks? How about now? If you obedience trained your dog, chances are he's learned a lot of important things since you first met. With this activity you can put on a show for your family and friends demonstrating all that your canine pal can do.

Materials
* 1 8½-by-11-inch piece of cardboard
* Pencil
* Scissors
* Construction paper
* Markers

Directions
Divide your show into three parts: obedience, tricks, and an obstacle course. In the obedience portion, include examples of all the instructions your dog follows, such as "sit," "stay," and "come." If your dog suffers from stage fright, you can do these tricks with him so he'll follow your lead. In the tricks portion, show all the cool stuff you and your dog can do, like fetch, roll over, sing, and shake. Finally, design an obstacle course where you can impress your family and friends with your dog's smarts (See Chapter 4 for a sample obstacle course). Once your program is set, you're ready to make your show program.

Fold the piece of cardboard in half so the short edges meet. On the front half of the cardboard, draw pictures of things your dog likes to play with, such as a bone, a ball, your cat, and you. Use the tip of the scissors to carefully puncture the cardboard and then cut out the shapes you've drawn. This is your stencil, or pattern, so you can make several programs.

Take a piece of construction paper and fold it in half so the short edges meet. Place this paper inside the stencil. Use a colored marker to trace the outline of the objects you've cut out of the cardboard onto the construction paper. Remove the construction paper and write on the program cover "Can-Do Canine Show," and include a date, time, and your dog's name (the star of the show!).

Open the construction paper. Draw a picture of you and your dog or another picture of things in your dog's life (such as your backyard) on one side. On the other side, write out the program you've chosen. Include the order of events. Make one program for each person who will be attending the show. Just before show time, set up some chairs and gather all the props you'll need for the performance, such as toys, chairs for the obstacle course, and treats to help reward your dog.

Tip
Give your dog a lot of praise during the show, and let her know she's doing a good job. This will help calm her down if she gets jumpy.

  ## Going to the Dogs

There are many occupations where you can work with animals. Here are just a few.

Animal shelter employee or volunteer

Animal trainer for TV and film

Kennel owner

Obedience trainer

Pet groomer

Pet-supply store owner

Pet sitter

Veterinarian

Veterinary assistant

Pet-assisted therapist, where you and a well-trained dog visit older citizens or people who are lonely

Can you think of others?

Reading List

These are animal books in The Anti-Cruelty Society's library of reading for children. Some titles are about dogs, such as *Beautiful Joe* by Marshall Saunders about a dog rescue, and some are about other animals, such as Cynthia Stowe's *Not-So-Normal Norman* about a boy who pet sits a tarantula. Some are collections of animal stories, like *James Herriot's Treasury for Children*.

Amber, A Very Personal Cat by Gladys Taber

Beautiful Joe by Quinn Currie (originally written by Marshall Saunders)

Big Red by Jim Kjelgaard

Black Beauty by Anna Sewell

Black Beauty by Quinn Currie (originally written by Anna Sewell)

Bonny's Big Day by James Herriot

Capyboppy by Bill Peet

Carl Goes Shopping by Alexandra Day

A Cat Called Christopher by Era Zistel

Cats Do, Dogs Don't by Norma Simon

Chickens Aren't the Only Ones by Ruth Heller

Cousin Charlie the Crow by Marshall Houts

The Dead Bird by Margaret Wise Brown

Do Animals Dream? Children's Questions About Animals Most Often Asked of the Natural History Museum by Joyce Pope

Dog Heaven by Cynthia Rylant

The Elephant's Child by Rudyard Kipling

The Faithful Friend by Lois Daniel

The Fall of Freddie the Leaf by Leo Buscaglia

Farewell to Shady Glade by Bill Peet

Father Goose and His Goslings by Bill Lishman

The Foundling by Carol Carrick

Four Black Puppies by Sally Grindley

Fudge by Charlotte Graeber

The Fur Person by May Sarton

The Golden Song by Jan Brincherhoff Chase

Good-bye My Friend by Mary Montgomery and Herb Montgomery

Harry Cat's Pet Puppy by George Selden

Harry the Dirty Dog by Gene Zion

Hawk, I'm Your Brother by Byrd Baylor

Hey! Get Off Our Train by John Burningham

Hunter and His Dog by Brian Wildsmith

I Never Met an Animal I Didn't Like by Rory C. Foster, D.V.M.

If a Seahorse Wore a Saddle by Mary Jane Flynn, M.D.

I'll Always Love You by Hans Wilhelm

James Herriot's Treasury for Children by James Herriot

Jim's Dog Muffins by Miriam Cohen

Joanna and Ulysses by May Sarton

Kenneth Lilly's Animals by Joyce Pope

Kids Can Save the Animals! 101 Easy Things to Do by Ingrid Newkirk

The Kid's Cat Book by Tomie De Paola

Kitty, the Raccoon by Jamie Stamper

Koko's Kitten by Dr. Francine Patterson

150

The Original Nanny

The original *Peter Pan* story by James M. Barrie tells how the Darlings were too poor to afford a human nanny so they bought a Newfoundland dog to keep an eye on the children. They named the dog Nana; hence, the first four-legged nanny came to be.

Resources

Animal-Friendly Television Networks

Animal Planet (AP) network
News, entertainment, documentary, and fiction about animals. Cable station.

My Pet TV
Pro-animal programs 24 hours a day. Cable station.

Puppy Channel
Still being test-marketed, this cable channel will air scenes of puppies playing with relaxing music. Viewers will submit the footage. The station will include pet product, care, and training information.

Organizations and Sponsored Events

American Humane Association (AHA)
63 Inverness Drive East
Englewood, CO 80112-5117
(800) 227-4645 or (303) 792-9900
www.americanhumane.org

Since 1877 this organization has worked for the protection and humane treatment of animals. It's a national federation of animal care, animal control agencies, and concerned individuals.

Since 1900 AHA has given the William O. Stillman Award to animals who, in the face of danger, have saved human lives as well as to humans who have rescued animals at great risk to themselves. So far more than 142 animals and 117 humans have received this national award.

Since 1915 AHA has sponsored Be Kind to Animals Week, the first full week every May, which features the Be Kind to Animals Kid Contest where winners are awarded college scholarships. Every kid who enters this contest receives a Certificate of Kindness from the AHA for caring about animals.

Kids between the ages of 6 and 13 can be nominated by local animal shelters or contact the AHA headquarters. The nominator must write, in 200 words or less, a description of how a kid has shown extraordinary kindness to animals and why he or she should be selected as the award winner. The nominator can submit photos, videos, or other supporting documentation.

On its Web site, AHA provides a listing of the latest national animal legislation.

American Kennel Club (AKC)
5580 Centerview Drive
Raleigh, NC 27606-3390
(919) 233-9767
www.akc.org/akc/

The American Kennel Club not only sponsors dog clubs throughout the United States, but it also provides public and canine education information, breeder references, and information on dog events in your area.

Junior Showmanship is a class of competition at dog shows for boys and girls between the ages of 10 and 18. Participants are judged on their handling of dogs in the show ring. Prizes are awarded to the young trainers who show the best skill in dog handling. The catch is that competing dogs must be AKC-registered purebreds.

The *AKC Jr. News* is the official quarterly newsletter for the AKC Junior Organization. To get a free subscription you need a junior dog handler number. Anyone who is between the ages of 10 and 18 can get a junior handler number by calling the number listed above.

American Society for the Prevention of Cruelty to Animals (ASPCA)
424 E. 92nd Street
New York, NY 10128
(212) 876-7700

The ASPCA sponsors the Adopt-a-Shelter-Dog Month every October, promoting the adoption of puppies and dogs from local shelters. For details send a SASE to the above address, or call the number above and ask for extension 4655.

The Anti-Cruelty Society
157 W. Grand Avenue
Chicago IL 60610
(312) 644-8338
Fax: (312) 644-3878
www.anticruelty.org

The Anti-Cruelty Society is a shelter in downtown Chicago that every year takes care of more than 16,000 animals and speaks to more than 40,000 schoolchildren to discuss taking care of pets responsibly.

People in the humane education department will answer questions on a variety of animal issues and provide follow-up materials for students, teachers, and the general public. Free educational materials are available for students in kindergarten through college. (You do not need to live in Chicago to receive these materials.)

People in the animal behavior and training department will answer behavior-related questions over the phone at no cost.

These resources and services are offered free of charge by The Anti-Cruelty Society, but because this organization receives no federal, state, or local government funding, they do request a donation.

They publish a quarterly catalog called the *ACS Boutique*, which offers many fun products for you and your dog or cat.

Center for Veterinary Medicine
Department of Health and Human Services
Food and Drug Administration
7500 Standish Place
Metro Park North 2
Rockville, MD 20855

Will send free information on dog and cat care.

The Humane Society of the United States
2100 L Street NW
Washington, DC 20037
(202) 452-1100
www.hsus.org

Promotes responsible pet ownership, fights animal cruelty and abuse, and is committed to helping solve pet problems before owners give up their pets. Children and teachers can contact the youth education division of The HSUS, the National Association for Humane and Environmental Education NAHEE), which publishes *KIND News*, a classroom newspaper. For more information write to NAHEE at P. O. Box 362, East Haddam, CT 06423, (860) 434-8666 or check out NAHEE on-line at www. nahee.org and *KIND News* at www.kindnews.org. A catalog of gift and care whose proceeds support Humane Society programs is available by calling (800) 486-2630.

National Mixed Breed Dog Clubs of America
and/or Linda Lewis
13884 State Route 104
Lucasville, OH 45648-8586
(740) 259-3941

Compete for titles in obedience, conformation, tracking, and more with your mixed-breed dog. All members receive a quarterly newsletter.

Here are some state-specific chapters of the mixed-breed dog club.

Mixed Breed Dog Club of California
c/o Christine Dane
1118 Marquita Avenue
Burlingame, CA 94010-3323

Mixed Breed Dog Club of St. Louis
c/o Stephanie Keough
233 Orchard Avenue
Winchester, MO 63021

Washington Mixed Breed Dog Club (Seattle area)
c/o Jim Laird
29350 N.E. Cherry Valley
Box 178
Duvall, WA 98019

Washington Mixed Breed Dog Club (Tacoma area)
c/o Theresa Zimmerman
3804 225th Street East
Spanaway, WA 98387

Raising Money for Pets Who Need Care

Many companies have programs to help pay for companion-animal programs or donate money to help support shelters. Here are just a few if you'd like to hold a fund-raiser.

Friskies PetCare Company, Inc.
Friskies Partners for Pets
Paws to Recycle!
800 N. Brank Boulevard
Glendale, CA 91203-1244
(800) 538-8327
www.Friskypet.com

Friskies was the recipient of the 1998 American Humane Association Special Achievement Award for its efforts to educate people about responsible pet care, to raise funds for animal shelters, and to encourage a national recycling program that provides additional money for animal welfare agencies. Contact Friskies for more information on how you or your classroom can lend helping hands to these efforts.

The makers of Alpo and Mighty Dog sponsor photo contests, calendar contests, and other prize-winning events and offers throughout the year. Check out their Web site for more details.

Heinz's Homeless Pet Program

Homeless Homer's Hotline
93 Albany Post Road
Montrose, NY 10548
(800) 842-4637

Clip and save the "Homeless Homer," Morris "Help Homeless Pets," or UPC symbols from Heinz pet-food products, and send them to the closest participating animal shelter (call the toll-free number to get the shelter's name and number). By collecting these symbols for participating shelters, you will help them receive a cash donation from Heinz Pet Products, which the shelter can use to help feed and care for their homeless pets. Started in 1981, this program has donated more than $3 million to local animal shelters and the American Humane Society.

Resources in an Emergency

Ani-Med Pet Care Information

(888) 252-7387
Developed by the American Society for the Prevention of Cruelty to Animals, this toll-free service offers prerecorded free information, 24 hours a day, 7 days a week, on more than 125 pet-care topics, such as how to deal with a dog who digs digging, ways to manage fleas, what to do when your dog is vomiting, how to find a veterinarian, and more. You'll receive five dollars worth of coupons every time you call

from some of the companies that sponsor this service, including Friskies, Pet Assure, EverFresh, HomeAgain, and others. Note: These are pre-recorded messages, so you cannot ask specific questions or get interactive help in an emergency.

ASPCA National Animal Poison Control Center

(800) 548-2423 or (888) 426-4435, $30 per case, payment by credit card only or (900) 680-0000, $20 for 5 minutes and $2.95 each minute thereafter.

Staffed by veterinarians and board-certified veterinary toxicologists, these hot lines provide animal poison and treatment information 24 hours a day. The toll-free numbers are a one-time-only service with the cost listed above. However, for the flat $30 rate plus toll fees, the center will make as many follow-up calls as necessary.

In the event of an emergency, be ready to provide your name, address, and phone number, the substance your animal was exposed to (if known), and descriptive details about the exposure, such as the amount of the substance eaten, how long ago, and so on. You will also need to tell them the species, breed, age, sex, weight, and number of animals involved. Finally, be ready to tell them the symptoms; that is, how your dog is behaving that worried you enough to call.

Pet First Aid

109 pages, $12.95

Coauthored by the American Red Cross and the Humane Society of the United States, this book tells you how to perform CPR on your pet, how to treat a wound until you can get your pet to a veterinarian, and more, whether you're at home or on the road with a dog or cat. This is an easy-to-understand guide to help you always be prepared for the unexpected.

It is available from HSUS at (800) 486-2630 (item number 52085) or the American Red Cross at (800) 337-2338.

Other Web Sites

American Pet Association

P.O. Box 18869
Boulder, CO 80308
(800) APA-PETS
Fax: (800) 258-PETS or

P.O. Box 725065
Atlanta, GA 31139-9065
Fax: (303) 402-1869
www.apapets.com
E-mail: APA@APAPETS.com, general information or Humane@APAPETS.com, humane services

Whether you're looking for help selecting the perfect pet, a veterinarian in your area, or help finding a lost dog, or if you just feel like challenging yourself with the American Pet Association (APA) on-line crossword puzzle, APA can be a helpful resource. These and other services can be accessed through their Web site or by contacting them over the phone. Some services do require a membership fee.

Animal Planet

www.animalplanet.com

Animal Planet offers updates on animal news from around the world, updated daily, and an easy way to search for specific types of programs, such as dog shows, *Lassie* episodes, and more. Of special note are the cameras that record the movements of some fascinating creatures, such as sea otters, sharks, and orangutans.

Cresthaven Kennels

www.cresthaven.com/books

Here's a site that recommends good dog books and videos. There are some listings for kids, such as the Lassie series videos and Lassie books. This site also has recommendations for books on health, nutrition, training, and more, but these are for more of an adult audience.

Dog Fancy On-Line

www.dogfancy.com

Publisher of a monthly magazine for dog lovers of all ages, this Web site includes a section called K-9 Kids—for responsible, caring kids who love their dogs. There are word scrambles; a way for you to send in your drawings, poetry, or essays about your canine friend; and a caption-writing contest.

This site also includes animal news stories, a list of suggested books by topic, a gift shopping area, and more.

Heinz Pet

www.heinzpet.com

You'll find information on this company's shelter support program and unique fun stuff, too. If you see a resemblance between you and your dog—Is the color or style of your hair the same? Do you have the same color eyes?—you can send a photograph of you and your dog to Heinz, and they may include it in their Animal Attraction subsite. A new subsite called Canine Comedians and Funny Felines is a place where you can share your dog or cat's silliness with others. Another area offers dog-training tips, such as how to teach a command called "go to bed" when your dog wants to play but you don't—like when you're doing your homework or talking on the phone.

How to Love Your Dog

www.howtoloveyourdog.com

Updated daily, this site features photographs and graphics from a family that owns three collies. This site offers information, dog book recommendations, safety tips, games, and much more for any young dog lover. It even offers instructions on how to save this Web site to your favorites list or how to make it your initial screen when you log on to the Web. This site is very kid-friendly.

Iams Pet Products

www.iams.com

This site features the Veterinarian's Corner, which offers an easy way to get answers to your pet-care questions. Iams is also sponsoring the Animal Planet's Trail to the Eukanuba Cup, a series of dog shows that will appeal to dog lovers and dog-show fans. The Iams Web site is updated regularly with tips for watching dog shows and a glossary of dog-show terms to help you follow the action. Animal Planet is a cable television station.

PetLife

www.petlifeweb.com

The magazine *PetLife* is published bimonthly and offers a lot of fun photos and tips for people and their pets. This Web site offers travel tips, a veterinarian to answer your questions and see the questions and answers of other readers, and an extensive list of companies that manufacture pet products.

Purina
www.Purina.com

This site features a lot of fun art where sometimes the dogs move across the screen. This site features some games, pet-care advice, a free puppy-care kit featuring Purina products, and more.

Real Dogs
www.realdogs.com

This site is still under construction (as of December 1998), but some areas are up and funny. In the dog-stories section you can read about the antics of other wonderful dogs and the people who love them. You can also add your own story and share how great your dog is with other readers.

Waltham World of Pet Care
www.waltham.com

This is filled with helpful information and fun. You'll find everything from tips to help you get the best photographs of your dog to first aid training tips. Their storyline provides dog stories for kids and includes color images, too.

X Marks the Spot
www.homearts.com/depts/pastime/petnam16.htm

This Web site helps you find the perfect name to describe your new pal, with suggestions from books, sports, cartoons, foods, and more.

Good Books to Have Around

Know Your Dog: An Owner's Guide to Dog Behavior
A veterinarian and author of more than 25 books about cats and dogs, Bruce Fogle knows a ton about these four-legged creatures. This is a practical handbook to help you recognize and interpret basic dog behavior. (See Bibliography for complete information.)

The Doctors Book of Home Remedies for Dogs and Cats
Edited by Matthew Hoffman, this book features care information from many pet professionals, including veterinarians, trainers, and breeders. This book will not only help you diagnose health problems and provide suggestions for when to see a professional, but it also features many home remedies for problems such as bad breath, ticks, and nonstop barking. (See Bibliography for complete information.)

Good News in the Mail or Mail-Order Specialists

Some of the organizations listed above offer catalogs of toys and treats (for example, The Humane Society of the United States). Here are a few more that specialize in mail-order delivery.

Doctors Foster & Smith

2253 Air Park Road
P.O. Box 100
Rhinelander, WI 54501-0100
(800) 826-7206

They offer a variety of leashes, treats, toys, and fun things for you to show you're a pet lover. You'll find some handy tips from veterinarians on the pages of this catalog, too.

The Dog & Cat Book Catalog

Direct Book Service
P.O. Box 2778
Wenatchee, WA 98807-2778
www.dogandcatbooks.com

Whether you check out their weekly updated Web site or wait for the catalog, you'll find books here for just you or for you to share with an adult, including books on training and behavior, specific dog breeds, health and nutrition; funny books; storybooks; videos; and more.

Help on the Road

Pets Welcome: A Guide to Hotels, Inns, and Resorts That Welcome You and Your Pet

Collected by Kathleen and Robert Fish, this directory lists places across the country where you and your pet can stay in comfort. Each location includes an address and phone number, room rates, whether they have a pet charge and how much, a paw rating for animal-friendliness, and a description of the accommodations. Five percent of the proceeds from the sale of this book go to The Humane Society of the United States.

Travel With or Without Pets: 25,000 Pets-R-Permitted Accommodations, Petsitters, Kennels & More!

Edited by M. E. Nelson and in its sixth edition, you know this is a good source for all kinds of options for pet-friendly travel. It is published by the Annenberg Communications Institute and available through Independent Publishers Group at (800) 888-4741.

Vacationing with Your Pet

Author Eileen Barish has compiled more than 20,000 pet-friendly lodgings in the United States and Canada. This book also offers tips on traveling safely with pets.

Bibliography

Books

American Kennel Club. *American Kennel Club Dog Care and Training*. New York: Howell Book House, 1991.

Benjamin, Carol Lea. *The Chosen Puppy: How to Select and Raise a Great Puppy from an Animal Shelter*. New York: Howell Book House, 1990.

de Baïracki Levy, Juliette. *The Complete Herbal Handbook for the Dog and Cat*. New York: Arco Publishing, Inc., 1985.

Comfort, David. *The First Pet History of the World*. New York: Fireside, 1994.

Encyclopaedia Britannica. 15th edition. Chicago: Encyclopaedia Britannica, 1997.

Evans, Mark. *Puppy: A Practical Guide to Caring for Your Puppy*. New York: Dorling Kindersley Limited, 1992.

Fogle, Bruce, D.V.M. *The Encyclopedia of the Dog*. New York: Dorling Kindersley Publishing, Inc., 1995.

Fogle, Bruce, D.V.M. *Know Your Dog: An Owner's Guide to Dog Behavior*. New York: Dorling Kindersley Publishing, Inc., 1992.

Gonzalez, Philip and Leonore Fleischer. *The Dog Who Rescues Cats: The True Story of Ginny*. New York: HarperCollins, 1995.

Hoffman, Matthew, editor. *The Doctors Book of Home Remedies for Dogs and Cats: Over 1,000 Solutions to Your Pet's Problems—from Top Vets, Trainers, Breeders, and Other Animal Experts*. Emmaus, Pennsylvania: Rodale Press, Inc., 1996.

Malone, John. *The 125 Most Asked Questions About Dogs [and the Answers]*. New York: William Morrow and Company, Inc., 1993.

McLennan, Bardi. *Dogs & Kids: Parenting Tips*. New York: Howell Book House, 1993.

Nyerges, Christopher. *Guide to Wild Foods and Useful Plants*. Chicago: Chicago Review Press, 1999.

Roach, Dr. Peter. *The Complete Book of Pet Care*. New York: Howell Book House, 1995.

Siegal, Mordecai. *A Dog for the Kids*. Boston: Little, Brown & Company, 1984.

Yaffe, Linda Frederick. *The Well-Organized Camper*. Chicago: Chicago Review Press, 1999.

Government Publications

Dzanis, David A., D.V.M., Ph.D. "Understanding Pet Food Labels." FDA Consumer, October 1994, pp. 11–15.

Farley, Dixie. "Fighting Fleas and Ticks." A reprint from *FDA Consumer* magazine, July–August 1996. Department of Health and Human Services, publication number (FDA) 96-6051.

Woods, Dr. Sandra. "Facts and Fallacies About Canine Immunization." Division of Therapeutic Drugs for Non-Food Animals, Center for Veterinary Medicine, Department of Health and Human Services, Food and Drug Administration, October 1985.

Woods, Dr. Sandra. "Information on Prevalent Tick-Borne Diseases." Division of Therapeutic Drugs for Non-Food Animals, Center for Veterinary Medicine, Department of Health and Human Services, Food and Drug Administration, September 1990.

Woods, Dr. Sandra. "One Dozen Nonchemical Ways to Control Canine Parasites." Division of Therapeutic Drugs for Non-Food Animals, Center for Veterinary Medicine, Department of Health and Human Services, Food and Drug Administration, November 1988.

Interviews

Baukert, Emil. D.V.M. Riser Animal Hospital. Interview by author. Skokie, IL. 8 June 1998.

Baukert, Mary. D.V.M. Skokie, IL. Interview by author. 24 August 1998.

Caruso, John. Humane Education Manager. The Anti-Cruelty Society, Society for the Prevention of Cruelty to Animals of Illinois. Interview by author. Chicago, IL. 10 April 1998.

Frank, Allan. Howard Street Animal Hospital. Interview by author. Chicago, IL. 18 May 1998.

Okura, Karen. Manager of Animal Behavior and Training. The Anti-Cruelty Society, Society for the Prevention of Cruelty to Animals of Illinois. Interview by author. Chicago, IL. 18 April 1998.

Weinman, Laura. Manager of Community Relations. Director of Advertising. The Anti-Cruelty Society, Society for the Prevention of Cruelty to Animals of Illinois. Interview by author. Chicago, IL. 10 April 1998.

Magazines

Hoofnagle, Laura. "Pest-Free, Naturally." *Conscious Choice.* November/December 1998, Volume 11, Number 6, p. 55.

Palika, Liz. "Social Graces," *Dog Fancy Magazine.* March 1992, pp. 8–14.

Pavia, Audrey. "Meet the AKC's Top Six," *Dogs U.S.A.* 1998 annual, pp. 12–18.

"Poisonous Plants for Your Pooch to Avoid," *Parade Magazine.* February 15, 1998.

Salzber, Kathy. "Brush Me Tender," *Puppies USA.* 1997–98, pp. 96–101.

Newsletters

"Growing Up," *Your Dog: A Newsletter for Dog Owners.* Tufts University School of Veterinary Medicine. Volume 1, Number 9, April 1995, pp. 1–3.

Newspapers

Kelley, Tina. "Advice from Vets and Other Experts," *The New York Times.* 10 September 1998, Midwest edition.

Kelley, Tina. "Every Dog Has Its Data," *The New York Times.* 10 September 1998, Midwest edition.

Acknowledgments

This book was a great adventure to write. I'd like to thank all the people who helped me along the way, including the good caring people at The Anti-Cruelty Society in Chicago and especially Karen Okura for her research help and her excellent feedback, John Caruso for his generosity and enthusiasm, and Laura Weinman for helping me connect to the right people. I'd like to thank Mary Baukert, D.V.M., Emil Baukert, D.V.M., and Allan Frank, D.V.M. I'd like to thank the very generous Peggy Johnson from The Lion and the Lamb. Thanks to Nancy Peterson, Martha C. Armstrong, and Danielle Jo Bays of The Humane Society of the United States. Thanks to Robin Allenbach, my chief treat taster Kirby, and Sandi Lawrence for providing Kirby's photo. Thanks and love to Dave, Gerie, and Olivia Greenspan and their precious dogs Zack and Garbo who can't get enough lovin' or treats.

I'd like to thank the whole gang at Chicago Review Press and Independent Publishers Group, but especially Cynthia Sherry, Linda Matthews, Yuval Taylor, Curt Matthews, and Mark Suchomel for giving me this opportunity. A special thanks goes to my project editor Rita Baladad for her diligence, thoughtfulness, and patience—skills that guided this manuscript into the beautiful and accessible book you now hold. Thanks to Bonnie Matthews whose adorable illustrations of real-looking kids and their dogs make this book so much fun to look at. Thanks to Mel Kupfer for her design and excellent step-by-step illustrations. Thanks to Gerilee Hundt for being a production goddess and keeping everything in line.

I'd like to thank William and Jean Hogarth for regularly checking on my progress and for their encouragement, and thanks to Bill and Sue

Hogarth for their help and to their daughters Alexandrea for her inspiration and Amanda just because. I'd like to thank my father for being such an enthusiastic cheerleader for this project. I'd like to thank the four-legged pals who enriched my life in the past including Peanut, Molly, Streak, Max, and Sundance. I'd like to thank Little One and Thumper, who gave me the space to write this book and often excused me from playtime. And most especially, I'd like to thank Ted Hogarth for supporting me, helping me, and encouraging me over this past year.